ERIE WRECKS
& LIGHTS

Georgann & Michael Wachter

Avon Lake, Ohio
March, 2007

This book is dedicated to our children

Brendon David Wachter and his wife Anja

Kimberly Wachter Petty and her husband Jason

and the memory of our daughter

Courtney Kristen Wachter

May 16, 1974 - January 30, 1993

ERIE WRECKS
& LIGHTS

Georgann & Michael Wachter

Cover painting by Georgann Wachter

ISBN: 978-0-9661312-5-3

Published by Corporate**Impact**
Avon Lake, Ohio
e-mail: shipwrecks@eriewrecks.com

ACKNOWLEDGEMENTS

We could not have produced this book without the help and encouragement of a great many people. In particular, we wish to express our appreciation to:

Christopher Gillcrist, Executive Director, Carrie Sowden, Archaeological Director; Noelle McFarland; and Tom Michaels, of the **Great Lakes Historical Society** in Vermilion, Ohio.

Bob Graham of **Historical Collections of the Great Lakes**, Center for Archival Collections, Bowling Green State University.

Eric Guerren, **Lakeshore Towing and Charters**, Erie, Pennsylvania.

Jim and Jimmy Herbert, **Osprey Dive Charters**, Barcelona, New York and Dunkirk, New York

Al Hart, Bay Village, Ohio provided access to his extensive collection of Great Lakes shipping information.

Larry and Mary Howard, Wrightsville, Pennsylvania have done what is perhaps the most extensive original research on eastern Lake Erie shipwrecks.

C. Patrick Labadie, Alpena, Michigan, author, researcher, historian, friend provided photos, invaluable information, and confirmation or rejection of some of our shipwreck identifications.

Jack Papes, Akron, Ohio, provided wonderful underwater images

Ralph Roberts: provided rare photos from his extensive private collection.

Rob Ruetschle, North Ridgeville, Ohio provided information on several pristine shipwrecks.

We also received information and assistance from the following individuals and institutions:

Erie County Historical Society, Erie Pennsylvania; Great Lakes Marine and U.S. Coast Guard Memorial Museum, Ashtabula, Ohio; Lower Lakes Marine Historical Society, Buffalo, New York; Rocky River Public Library, Rocky River, Ohio; Rutherford B. Hayes Memorial Presidential Center, Fremont, Ohio; Sandusky Maritime Museum, Sandusky, Ohio.

Rod Althaus of Port Clinton, Ohio; Brendon Baillod of Marshal, Wisconsin; John Davis of Williamsville, New York; Carl Engel of Painesville, Ohio; Harry Goodman of New Bern, North Carolina; Ed & Riki Herdendorf of Sheffield Village, Ohio; Wayne Hopper of Belmont, Ontario; Allen King of Lemington, Ontario; Doug King of Blasdell, New York; Tom Kowalczk, Lakeside, Ohio; Gary Kozak of Derry, New Hampshire; Gerald MacDoanald of Port Maitland, Ontario; Kevin McGee of Cleveland, Ohio; Gerry and Walter Paine of Avon Lake, Ohio; Jim Paskert of Medina, Ohio; Alice Peron of Clayton, New York; Roy Pickering of Erieau, Ontario; Larry Slomski of Sagertown, Pennsylvania; Pat and Jim Sterling of Toledo, Ohio; Tom Wilson of New Market, Ontario; Craig Workman of Port Colborne, Ontario; David VanZandt of Lakewood, Ohio; Ron Yanega of Perry, Ohio.

DISCLAIMER

The authors have made every effort to assure the accuracy of the contents of this book. However, no warranty is expressed or implied that the information contained in this volume is accurate or correct. In fact we expect to hear from many people pointing out errors in our facts! The authors shall in no way be responsible for any consequential, incidental, or exemplary loss or damage resulting from the use of any of the graphics or printed information contained in this book. The authors disclaim any liability for omissions, errors, or misprints and give notice to all readers that this book is not to be used for dive planning or navigation.

Some of the shipwrecks described in this volume are beyond the limits of sport diving as defined by all major certifying agencies. They should only be attempted by very experienced divers with specialized training and equipment for depths in excess of sport diving limits.

INTRODUCTION

"There is a captain sailing the lakes who don't know the taste of whisky, and who neither smokes nor chews. He does not hail from Cleveland, however."

- June 29, 1882, *Cleveland Plain Dealer.*

Our winters are devoted to research where we learn the written stories behind the shipwrecks, and find great quotes like the one above. Summers are spent on the boat.

As we hopscotch around Lake Erie, another lighthouse looms over a port; a sentinel greeting mariners and enduring the tempestuous storms of Mother Nature. For some these beacons have been a welcome sight, even a means of salvation. For others they have lit a terrifying scene; a maelstrom of water inundating a breakwall and alabaster rocks ready to impale a ship.

Once ashore, we check out the harbor and people. Wandering the pier, we hear stories from both residents and transients. They narrate tales of the boats, families, and towns. Asked why we are there, we say, "To find and dive shipwrecks." Some shrug in disinterest. Most express incredulous curiosity and excitement. They probe us with cautious questions.

Lake Erie's harbors have made us many friends.

By day we explore a new piece of water. At night we sit by a fire or in a cramped boat cabin, gleaning information that was not in the newspapers or official reports. We hear of a vessel wrecked on a nearby shore, while images of another boat that foundered on the same day off another port flood our minds. Connecting the dots around the lake, we realize that several vessels were often torn apart in the same tempest. These steamers, schooners, tugs, and barges share a frightening history.

So we gather the stories as the sun sets benignly behind the lighthouse towers. Along the way we hatch a few adventures of our own. The following pages tell these sagas and provide a glimpse of the fascination many of us have for shipwrecks, lighthouses, and the great storms of the past centuries.

This 1930s postcard shows the light that once marked the entrance to the Portage River at Port Clinton. Today the river mouth is marked by simple lights, atop skinny poles. However, the old light still stands at Brand's Marina. Postcard from authors' collection.

CONTENTS

Lighthouses of Lake Erie _____ 48

Shipwrecks _____ 110

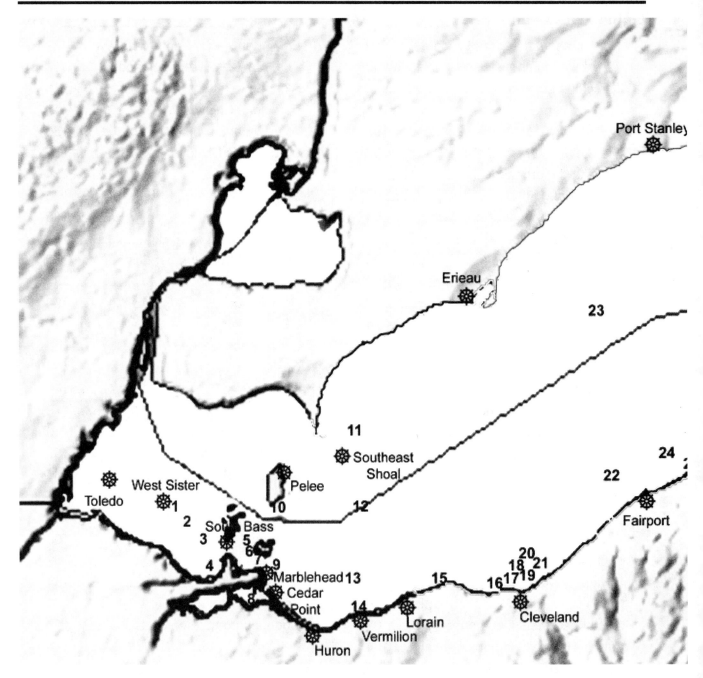

1	Custodian	11	Adams, E.S.
2	Wisconsin	12	Commodore
3	Chicago Board of Trade	13	Vermilion Small Barge
4	Detroiter	14	Sugar Barge
5	Constitution	15	King Coal
6	Crocker, L.B.	16	Bradstreet's Disaster
7	Plummer, C.H.	17	Gold Coast Tug
8	Stafford, W.R.	18	Merick, M.F.
9	Barlum, John J.	19	Lakewood Tug
10	Carroll, J.J.		

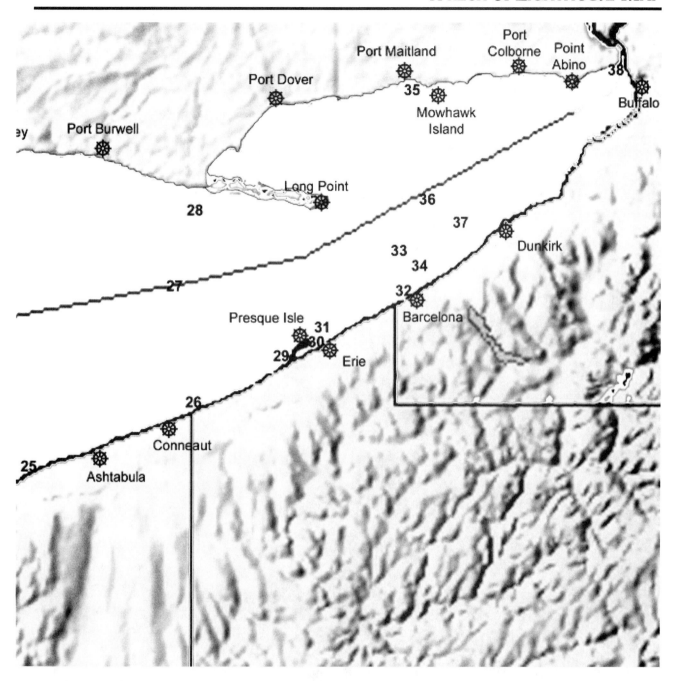

20 Cleveland Crib	29 Patapsco
21 CSU Wreck	30 Hammermill Wreck
22 Ogdensburg	31 Rob Roy
23 Perry, Theodore	32 Mautenee
24 ESCO #2	33 Whelan, George J.
25 Red Bird	34 Barcelona Shipwreck
26 Algerine	35 Maitland Railroad Cars
27 Mitchell, Belle	36 Admiralty Wreck
28 Caterpillars	37 Brig "C"
	38 International

THE GREAT STORMS

A whaleback steamer in heavy water. Photo from Great Lakes Historical Society

In researching Great Lakes shipwrecks, we were struck by the carnage one storm could produce. Shallow Lake Erie, with its northeast/southwest orientation, often bares the brunt of the weather patterns that sweep across the North American continent from the southwest. While maximum waves from these tempests are smaller than on the other Great Lakes, the short trough between sets made one Atlantic Ocean captain we met, scurry for shelter in nine foot seas. In addition, sustained winds from the southwest or northeast cause water to pile up at one end of the lake and empty at the other. The seiche associated with this effect may be as much as ten feet in height.

The most severe weather seems to be born from Gulf of Mexico hurricanes that generally occur in October or November. There were other storms that were as severe as those we chose to include in this

Lake Erie with 35 to 40 m.p.h. winds in October 2006. Authors' photo

book. For example, there were back-to-back gales in mid to late October of 1870. However, these did not produce as many human casualties, in part because the vessels involved were schooners with smaller crews. There is also less information available on earlier storms because the newspapers of the day (1800s) were often only four pages long and were published once a week, rather than daily.

We have tried to sort out conflicting stories, misspelled names, and differing casualty reports. Unfortunately, the itinerant nature of a seaman's life creates a situation where sailors were often added to a vessel's crew without notice to company agents. Missing log books that went down with shipwrecks make it so no record of a ship's compliment survived the incident. It was also common for a "river rat" from the wharfs not to reveal his true name. Add to this the practice of having unexpected or unreported passengers on board, such as wives, girlfriends, and stowaways; getting an accurate listing of casualties is virtually impossible.

One could rank storms by the number of casualties produced. This ranks the October 1893 storm (53 lives lost) as the most severe. It would be followed by the December 1909 storm (51 lives lost) and the 1916 Black Friday storm (50 lives lost) as the most vicious tempests on Lake Erie. However, for all the reasons noted above, we know our lists are probably not completely correct.

The crews who suffered through, and survived, torrents of water, sleet and blasting cold winds in any of these storms would tell you that their ordeal was the worst. Having experienced Lake Erie's twelve to fifteen foot waves in a thirty-seven foot boat, we would not argue with them. Only they can truly know the terror or valor of their mates as men lived or died on the lake.

THE OCTOBER 14 STORM OF 1886

Remnants of a hurricane from the Gulf of Mexico brought "wreck and woe" to the Great Lakes in October of 1886. The wind driven water that drowned hundreds in Texas, Louisiana, and Arkansas roared up through the Midwest, reaching Lake Erie on Wednesday, October the thirteenth. The storm began at gale force, with thirty to forty mile per hour south winds. By the evening, the winds had increased to a full storm with fifty-five to sixty-five m.p.h. winds out of the southwest. The first vessels to be affected were plying the west end of the lake on October 14th. The schooner *Sea Lark* plowed into Pelee Island, and the schooner *Saint Joseph*, in ballast, also hit the southern point of Lake Erie's largest island.

The W.R. Hanna

The total loss of the scow *W.R. Hanna* was not even noted until two weeks after the event. The scow/schooner *Hanna* was owned by Captain Frank Provonsha of Toledo. The 29 year old vessel was loading stone at Kelleys Island North Dock, when she was torn from her moorings and driven eastward, across North Bay to crash upon the rocks. Her uninsured hull never reached the intended destination of Detroit. Today, she still lies on the bottom at the eastern side of Kelleys Island's North Bay.

See *Erie Wrecks West* for additional information on this shipwreck.

Artifacts recovered from the *W.R. Hanna*

Wreck ashore. Great Lakes Historical Society Bowen Collection

The O.M. Bond

The Lakes had done their best to claim the *O.M. Bond* early in the season of 1886. The wreckers had spent more than four months working to repair the schooner, which had sunk in May off Point Dalhousie on Lake Ontario. It was an unhappy coincidence that she would begin her first voyage after the rebuild just as the October storm reached Lake Erie.

Captain Peter Lefevere, owner and master of the *Bond*, survived the wreck to recount the disaster. He reported that the *O.M. Bond* left Detroit on Thursday bound to Buffalo with a cargo of wheat. A strong wind was encountered from the south as the vessel entered Lake Erie, so the sails were reefed. With little warning, the wind blew violently from the west, causing the schooner to roll and shift her cargo. Unable to steer, the *Bond's* crew watched helplessly as she was driven on the beach about four miles above Rondeau Light.

The vessel was now swept by towering seas, which forced the crew into the rigging. The mainmast began to cant wildly to one side, so Captain Lefevere ordered all hands to the foremast. All but three of the crew complied. Using the fore boom for guidance, the captain, cook, and three others attained the crosstrees of the foremast. Mate Patrick Ryan and seaman James Hughs disregarded the captain's warning that the mainmast would fall to port. They were swept into the sea and drowned when it

Wreck of Old Schooner Found On Erie Shore

Found East of Rondeau Harbor. Could these be the remains of the *O.M. Bond*? *London Free Press* October 8, 1960.

A WEEK OF WOE.

Dire Disasters That Have Overtaken Unfortunate Humanity.

Work of the Wind and Flood.

Many Lives Lost and Great Destruction of Property.

Casualties on Land and Sea.

Further Particulars of the Sabine Pass Horror—Over Fifty Persons Known to Have Been Drowned—The Propeller Selah Chamberlain Sunk in Collision With the Pridgeon on Lake Michigan and Five of the Crew Go Down With the Wreck—The Schooner George M. Case Founders Off Port Colborne—Her Captain and One Sailor Perish—A Great Storm on the Lakes and Throughout the Entire West—Fearful Fires in Maine and Indiana—Other Calamities.

The *Cleveland Plain Dealer* proclaimed The October 1886 storm to be a "Week of Woe".

crashed into the fore rigging. One plucky sailor, who stayed on the main mast, got tangled in the rigging but freed himself by cutting off his boot. He somehow managed to get to the fore rigging. Hours later, a man living nearby braved the storm and rowed his skiff to the rescue.

The area west of Rondeau has been searched by the authors and by others for remains of the *O.M. Bond*. Unusual carved formations of mud, rising ten or more feet off the bottom have made it so any possible remains of the *Bond* are still undetected.

The George M. Case

Until the completion of the new Welland Canal in 1884, vessels had to be no larger than 140 feet long by 26.5 feet wide to passage the canal between Lake Erie and Lake Ontario. The October 14th Storm was particularly hard on canal sized schooners. The canaler *George M. Case* was completed by master builder John B. Martel for her owners Conger and Case of New York. She had a straight stem and her

George M Case. Photo from Authors' collection

Sophia Minch aground at Ashtabula near where the *Nevada* went ashore. The *Sophia Minch* was recovered. Authors' collection.

dimensions were intended to maximize cargo through the Welland Canal. By 1884, she was captained and owned by William McDonald of Chicago. In the fall of 1885, a storm on Lake Michigan dismasted and almost destroyed the *Case*. By the spring of 1886 she had been rebuilt. Toward the end of the season she left Chicago, packed with corn, for Buffalo. The vessel would never reach her destination.

On October the 14th, "Buffalo was almost blown away" by the October Storm. Southwest winds had increased to 63 miles per hour and raised water at the east end of the lake some eight feet.

The leaky *George M. Case* had a substitute captain, William Dailey, who was relieving owner Captain McDonald due to his being ill. As the schooner neared Port Colborne, she foundered. Bravely, the tugs *Routh* and *Moore* set out to the site. They managed to rescue four men who were clinging to the spars. Captain Dailey, cook Maggie Kreiden, and sailor Ole Green perished.

Captain McDonald was planning to rejoin his crew in Buffalo when he received word that his vessel was gone. The final resting place of the *George M Case* was reported to be 3 to 8 miles southwest of Port Colborne in seven fathoms of water.

Crew of the *Belle Mitchell's* sister ship *Oliver Mitchell* prepares to set sail. Authors' collection.

The Nevada

Certainly, the twenty year old schooner *Nevada* had weathered many a blow. Unfortunately, the October Storm found her in the wrong storm at the wrong time. The canal sized vessel, built and still owned in Oswego, New York, was lucky in some respects as her entire crew escaped with their lives. At 1:30am, the *Nevada* was upbound with a cargo of coal when the storm's huge seas cast her on the beach five miles below (east of) Ashtabula. Her crew watched as two small boats were overturned attempting to mount a rescue. The lifesavers suddenly had become victims of the hurricane. Fortunately, they were pulled from the water by local tugs. With the hope of salvation suddenly torn away, the men may have succumbed to the tortuous waves, but along came the bark *C.B. Benson* with her experienced owner and Captain, John Duff. His crew manned a boat that was able to rescue the sailors of the *Nevada*.

Stranded, with her canvas torn by the gale and her bottom wearing on the rocks, the ship's owner, John Martin, was glad to be insured. In the next couple of days, what was left of the schooner *Nevada* was advertised for sale. The newspapers used this incident to champion a lifesaving station for Ashtabula Harbor. In 1893, one was established at that port.

Wheel and steering mechanism of the *Belle Mitchell*. Video capture by the authors.

The Belle Mitchell

Large quantities of flotsom and jetsom were tossed up on the Erie, Pennsylvania peninsula from this storm. Some of it undoubtedly belonged to the schooner *Nevada,* which was pounding on the coast near Ashtabula, some thirty-five miles away. However it was the two masted schooner *Belle Mitchell* that suffered the most in the storm of October 14, 1886. Her entire crew was lost. Relatives of the crew conducted an extensive search for their missing loved ones. (This story is told in detail in the shipwrecks section of this book.)

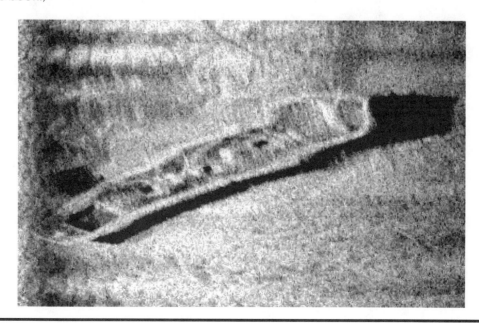

A Tormented Lake in October 1893

The Dean Richmond

Captain Jack Tierney of the steamer *W.H. Stevens* swore as he watched the laboring railroad steamer *Dean Richmond*. The wind was blowing at almost

never turned back for a storm yet and I never will.' " (*Cleveland Leader,* October 24, 1893).

The boat left Toledo at 5pm on Friday the thir-

This drawing of the *Dean Richmond* appeared in the *Toledo Evening Bee* 10-16-1893..

60 miles per hour, and he was hoping to get his vessel safely to Erie, Pennsylvania. Now, some four miles east of Erie, he sighted the *Richmond* missing one of her stacks. With the next heave of the sea, the other stack and spar cascaded over her rails. The *Dean* was in trouble in the trough of the furious waves, but Captain Tierney's first duty was to his own crew. He turned his steamer and returned to Buffalo.

The *Dean Richmond* was a package freighter under charter to the Cloverleaf Railroad. She carried rail freight between Toledo, Ohio and Buffalo, New York. Her captain, G.W. Stoddard, had been the porter on the vessel when she made her first trip in 1864. Now, forty years later, he commanded the *Richmond*.

The *Toledo Commercial* recounted, "While waiting for his clearance papers the afternoon before the *Richmond* started for Buffalo, (by) strange coincidence, the subject of storms on the lakes was broached … Captain Stoddard said grimly, 'I've

teenth with a cargo of 2,550 barrels of flour, four cars of oilcake, three cars of meal, spelter (zinc ingot), pig lead, and seventy-seven carloads of package freight. The last boat to observe the *Dean* was the steamer *Neosho* who reported her location as forty miles from Buffalo. The *Neosho* confirmed the *W.H. Stevens* report that her stacks were down, and she seemed to be having trouble with her steering gear. This sighting was on Saturday.

In the early morning of Sunday, October 15th, farmer Frank Boling of Dunkirk, New York, went out to view the carnage of the storm. In a mess of wreckage and flour paste, he found the bodies of Andrew Dodge, crewman from the galley, and Walter Goodyear, the *Richmond's* first mate. Goodyear's watch was stopped at 12:20, fixing the time the *Richmond* had lost the struggle with the lake at 12:20am on Sunday. Eight miles further east, Captain Stoddard's body, encased in a life jacket, was found. His watch had a woman's picture on the dial, and the hands also read 12:20.

Neal Dow as a 10 year old watched debris come ashore from the *Dean Richmond*. Before moving, he worked for a time as a cartoonist for the *Dunkirk Observer*. This cartoon was mocking one of the treasure searchers looking for the *Dean*.

Found wondering aimlessly on the beach was C.L. Clarke, who said he shipped on the freighter at Toledo. He recounted that the captain's wife and three children were locked in the cabin for safety as the waves ran over the decks. Finally, the captain decided to beach the vessel. As Clarke readied the yawl boat, he was washed overboard. However, Mr. Clarke's tale turned out to be a cruel hoax. The only female on board was stewardess Mrs. Retta Ellsworth, and certainly none of the captain's family was on that fatal voyage.

One man of the *Richmond's* crew did come ashore alive. Lookout Exie Wheeler had struggled to the beach west of Dunkirk, removed his life vest, and climbed out of the surf zone. Then he died. When his father came to claim his young son's body, he asked about a watch that had been a present to his son the previous Christmas. It was established that the watch found in Walter Goodyear's pocket belonged to Exie.

On Monday, three men from the town of Sheridan, New York went out in a small boat in search of bodies. When their vessel overturned, their lives were added to the storm's toll.

Chief Engineer G.F. Hogan was part owner of the cursed vessel. He had decided to attend the Chicago World's Fair and had recruited a nephew, Frank H. Hilton to take his place. He hurried from his home in Port Huron to identify the eighteen crew lost on the *Dean Richmond*.

Over time, rumors grew that the *Dean Richmond* carried ingots of copper, not pig lead. Treasure hunters combed the lake looking for her remains. Meanwhile the father of Frank and Jacob Earnest also hoped the wreck would be found. He wanted to remove their bodies from that watery tomb.

Additional information on the *Dean Richmond* is in *Erie Wrecks East*.

The Wocoken

Captain John Mitchell was sitting in his Cleveland office in the Perry Payne Building worrying about his steamer, *Wocoken*. That morning he had read the awful news about the foundering of the steamer *Dean Richmond*, a vessel he had

This Neal Dow cartoon seeks to blame the removal of her hogging arches for the loss of the *Dean Richmond*.

sailed upon. He was painfully digesting the news that he would never again see his friends, the *Richmond's* captain and crew, when he received a telegram stating that the *Wocoken's* consort, the schooner *Joseph Paige*, was laying in shelter under Long Point. But his worst fears were realized when a second telegram, posted from Port Rowan, Ontario, arrived. Penned by second mate J.P. Saph, it read, "Captain John Mitchell, Cleveland: Wocoken gone. All dead except Robt. Crowding of Delaware, J.H. Rice & myself." (*The Evening Post*, Cleveland, October 17, 1893).

John Mitchell and his brother, Captain Alfred, had more to grieve about than the loss of one of Mitchell & Company's ships and crew. Their only sister, Sarah, was sailing on the steamer with her husband, Captain Albert Meswald.

Leaving Ashtabula, Ohio on Friday the 13th, Captain Meswald and crew made a quick trip to Erie, Pennsylvania to pick up their consort, the coal laden schooner *Joseph Paige*. Tempting fate again, both vessels departed Erie at noon on the thirteenth. Their intended destination was Duluth, Minnesota. The water was placid at first as the tow headed upbound, though it was not long before the wind shifted to the northeast and it began to rain. By Saturday morning, a terrific wind was blowing at 55 miles per hour from the northwest. The steamer and her consort were not able to make headway in the heavy seas. Mate Saph reported,

"It was blowing hard, so hard we could hardly stand on deck... We kept the *Wocoken* headed into the wind. Then, she turned on us and played into the trough of the sea, dunnage, yawl boats, water barrels were scattered. We threw the dunnage overboard so it wouldn't tear our hatch cloths... The sea became larger and began to sweep over the deck. Mrs. Meswald was in the aft cabin where she could not hear the roar of the wind or sea. Fearing the cabin would get washed off, I told the captain he better go back and get his wife. We both carried Mrs. Meswald up forward into his room... I went forward, Henry Krantz came and told me the cabin washed in and steam pipes were broken. The engineers stood by until the sea drove them out of the engine room.

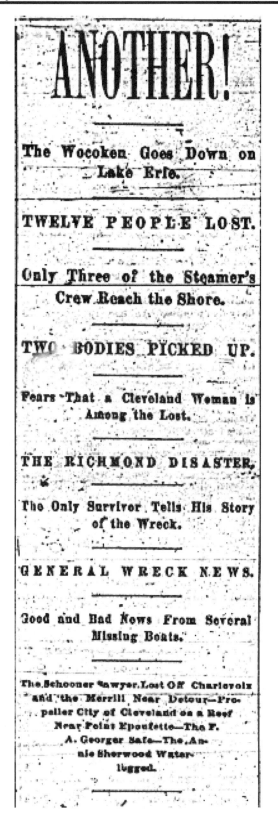

Cleveland Leader, October 16, 1893

"By now the *Wocoken* had turned and was being pushed before the towering seas. The schooner consort was released as the steamer drifted toward the sand hills. Three deckhands took to a small boat … but they had to be rescued. The water started to foam on deck and I knew it would be soon she would go down…

"I had to go down on deck and meet Henry Krantz. I told him we better take to the riggings, as Henry started ahead of me he was washed overboard, also the pilot house and Texas, carrying the entire crew overboard, including Captain Meswald and his wife.

"By the time the sea struck us the *Wocoken* was on the bottom, the water half covering me, I got high enough on the rigging and looked around. I saw nothing, no cry, no sound, only the roar of the sea. I climbed to the crosstree where two other men were" (A Great Lakes Saga).

When Captain Meswald's body was found, his gold watch had stopped at 10:45pm on Saturday. It was not until 4:30 in the afternoon on Sunday that lifesavers from Port Rowan labored for four hours to reach the half dead sailors stranded on the *Wocoken's* foremast.

The steamer's consort, the *Paige*, managed to raise her sails and get into shelter behind Long Point. By the time she reached the bay, her sails were in tatters, and she had five feet of water in her hold. The tug *Scott* eventually towed her into Buffalo.

Seventeen perished on the *Wocoken*, including; fifteen year old Harry Oleson who had run away from Milwaukee on the *Massachusetts* but was returning home on the *Wocoken*.

Mrs. Cynthia Mitchell at once joined part owner Phillip Morris and her son Alfred in Erie, seeking the body of her daughter Sarah. A reward of $200 was offered. Several bodies were located, including Captain Albert Meswald's, but Sarah Meswald's remains were never found.

Steamer *Wocoken*.

A diver sent to the wreck of the *Wocoken*, two miles off Clear Creak, Ontario, reported that nothing remained but her bottom and scattered piles of coal from her cargo.

For additional information on the *Wocoken*, see *Erie Wrecks East*.

RIVERSIDE GIVEN UP.

BELIEVED TO HAVE GONE DOWN NEAR PT. PELEE.

Capt. M. J. Farrington, First Mate Joseph Hargrove and Seaman John Hargrove, His Son, All Detroiters Among the Lost.

All hope of again seeing the schooner Riverside and her crew of seven has been abandoned. Eight days ago this morning she left port, and since then not the faintest definite trace of her whereabouts has been found. It is thought by some that the spars seen sticking out of water below Point Pelee belong to the lost schooner.

All the lists heretofore published of the victims of the Riverside wreck are wrong. William Raymond, seaman, reported lost, called at the office of Capt. J. M. Jones, owner of the boat, yesterday, and denied emphatically

(CAPT. JOSEPH HARGROVE.)
Mate of the lost schooner Riverside.

Cleveland *Evening News*, October 19, 1893

The Riverside

William Raymond came calling at the office of Captain J.M. Jones, owner of the schooner *Riverside*. His mission was to declare that he was not dead! In fact, another crewman of the *Riverside*, William Whelan, had also left the ship at Kelleys Island, where she had loaded stone for what would be her final voyage. Her full load of 670 tons of limestone would never reach Tonawanda, New York. Like the *Wocoken*, she sailed on Friday the thirteenth, and she just didn't arrive. The Canadian steamer *Cuba* did sight three persons mid-lake in a yawl boat on Saturday the fourteenth. Being disabled herself, the *Cuba* was unable to assist them.

Captain David Farrington, of Picton, Ontario, had brought along his wife as the cook. They left their daughter, Eunice, with his parents. As co-owners of the Riverside, Farrington and his cousin, John Hargrove, had persuaded John's father, Captain Joseph Hargrove, to leave his retirement of thirteen years and the comfort of his farm in order to sail on the recently purchased schooner.

The remains of the schooner *Riverside* were located in October of 1893 because her spars, ornamented with gilt balls, were protruding from the water. A total of seven lives were lost when she went down. More recently, scuba divers located her in 85 feet of water, over 25 miles northwest of Cleveland. She has two woodstock anchors and a very unusual hinged bowsprit. The brass bell and a very nice wheel are still on the wreck. There are two masts missing and the third mast is broken twenty four feet above the deck. The cabin is still attached and the portholes are in place. For obvious reasons, this location has not been released.

The C.B. Benson

"Gone, The Famous Schooner *C.B. Benson* ... No better known craft on the lakes"

So read the headlines of the Toledo, Ohio papers in October 1893.

The *C.B. Benson* was built in 1873/1874 in Port Clinton, Ohio by Captain John Duff, who was the only master this bark ever had. Almost immediately after her launch, she was commissioned to carry a load of corn to Cork, Ireland. Her victorious arrival in Queenstown (Cork) was heralded in the July 17, 1874 *Chicago Inter Ocean*, which declared it; "the inauguration of Our Lake European Trade." The article went on to scorn a recent report in the New York *Bulletin* that had been sceptical of the "frail" lake craft's voyage. For the next three years, the *Benson* called on ports in the British Isles and South America before returning permanently to the Great Lakes.

Captain John Duff was a well respected seaman who fed his family by sailing the lakes. He earned accolades for saving the crew of the schooner *Nevada*, which broke up on the Ashtabula, Ohio coastline in October of 1886. He and his family spent the winter of 1892 building yet another vessel at their home in Port Clinton.

By the season of 1893, John Duff was sixty-four

years old. His second son, Curtis, had been appointed mate. In the fall, Curtis' wife, Carrie Duff, had decided not to sail with her husband and father-in-law because she was pregnant and often felt ill. On October 7, the *Benson* was docked in Buffalo Harbor, and Curtis wrote to Carrie. In his letter, he mentioned that the run from Toledo to Buffalo with a cargo of grain had been smooth sailing. However, it was now blowing a gale. In fact, he stated, "The wind was so high last night that the water was over the top of the dock where the tug lays. I didn't think it got so high down here."

Unable to secure a cargo in Buffalo, the *Benson* sailed to Erie, Pennsylvania, where John Duff posted a card to his wife who, like her daughter-in-law, was named Carrie. In the card, John explained he could not get a cargo that would take him home to Toledo, so instead, the eight man

C.B. Benson at Oswego. Photo from Gerry Duff Paine.

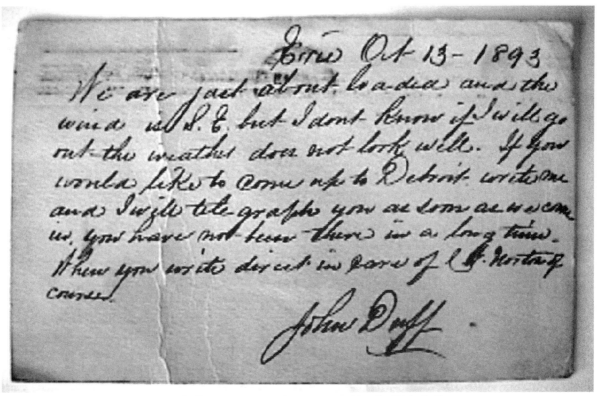

John Duff's last and prophetic message to his wife Carrie Duff.

crew was loading coal for Detroit. He mentioned that First Mate Fred Amgo had missed the sailing in Buffalo so came to Erie by rail to meet the schooner. Duff also lamented that it was hard to get crew.

On Friday, October 13th John sent a second postcard to Carrie Duff. He wrote, "We are just about loaded and the wind is S.E. but I don't know if I will go out – the weather does not look well." This foreboding message would be the experienced captains last. Captain Duff ignored his instincts and started on the voyage. The C.B. *Benson* was last seen off Port Stanley late on Friday the thirteenth by the Steamer *State of Ohio*. She was running back under head sails. Then she went missing.

On Sunday, October 15th, several merchantmen reported the topmasts of a vessel sticking out of the water near Port Colborne, Ontario. These masts were painted black and to one was fastened an oil cloth signal of distress. At first, it was widely reported that the missing schooner *F.C. Leighton* was the sunken vessel. Then, someone remembered that the *Leighton* had light colored topmasts. A couple of other overdue boats were suspected as being the wreck off Gravely Bay. Finally, on

Carrie Duff. Photo courtesy Jerry Duff Paine.

Wednesday the eighteenth, the *C.B. Benson* was identified as lost with Captain Duff, his son Curtis, Mate Amgo, the cook, and four seamen.

John Duff's run for the safety of the lea of Long Point had ended unsuccessfully sometime on October 14th. Thus began an eerie tradition, as two other schooners owned by the Duff family came to grief on October 14th. These were the *Nellie Duff* that sank off Lorain, Ohio on October 14, 1895, and the *Kate Winslow* that foundered in Lake Huron on October 14, 1897.

The *Cleveland Leader* was quoted in the October 28, 1893 *Sandusky Register*, "No bodies have been found on the beach near the wreck of the *Benson*, but this is not strange as not a single body of the crew of the *J.D. Finney*, which went down last fall in the same spot, was ever recovered. There was no better seaman on the lakes than Captain Duff, and he had every confidence in his schooner."

Unfortunately, neither experience nor a stout ship was an adequate adversary for the storm of October 13 to 15 of 1893. In 1894, a little boy named Curtis Duff was born to Carrie Duff. He was named after a father he would never know.

John Duff

See *Erie Wrecks East* for additional information on the *C.B. Benson*.

This hurricane also wrecked havoc on Lakes Huron, Michigan, and Superior and tore into the New England states. On October 14, the wind at Buffalo was sixty-one miles per hour and the barometer read 28.156. The wind was so strong at the Toledo end of Lake Erie, that people could walk across the valley created by the Maumee River. The loss of life was set a fifty, plus the three would be rescuers lost in the small boat from Sheridan, New York.

Wheel of the *C.B. Benson*. Video capture by the authors.

The October 19 & 20 Storm of 1905

It was certainly an ill wind that blew across the Great Lakes on October 19 and 20 of 1905. Casualties were high on Lakes Michigan, Superior, Huron, and Erie. More than thirty boats were seriously damaged or totally lost. Six vessels would never sail again on Lake Erie.

The Tasmania

Captain James Corrigan was concerned, but confident that his sailors were cared for when he heard reports that at least one of his salmon-colored fleet vessels had gone down near Southeast Shoal. Unfortunately, the spars standing out of the shallow water at the west end of Lake Erie marked the graves of eight men.

The schooner barge *Tasmania* was built in 1871 as a mammoth 221 foot sailing vessel with four masts, called the *James Couch*. After many years of service, she was converted to a barge, and two masts were removed.

Schooner *Tasmania*

It was eleven o'clock on Thursday, October 19th when a violent storm overtook the Corrigan steamer *Bulgaria* and her consorts, the *Ashland* and *Tasmania*. As the storm's fury increased, Captain Arthur Adams of the barge *Ashland*, had his men batten the cabin windows so the water tearing along the decks would not break the glass. The *Ashland*, in the center of the convoy, was being constantly tugged at both ends by the larger vessels *Bulgaria* and *Tasmania*. Oilskins were no match for the frigid waters as Captain Adam's men clung for dear life on deck. About 5am on Friday, the Captain reported, "Suddenly I felt the tow line from the *Tasmania* tugging hard as the *Bulgaria* tried to tow us on. I knew in a minute that the *Tasmania* had foundered, and I cut the rope." (*Cleveland Plain Dealer*, October 22, 1905)

Captain William Radford of Courtright, Ontario and seven sailors had drowned.

The *Ashland's* captain alleged there was nothing anyone could do to rescue the *Tasmania's* crew in the raging storm. Yet, he insisted if the barge's sailors had climbed the masts, they would have been saved. Bitter relatives of the *Tasmania's* captain felt that the vessel foundered after, and because, the tow line was severed by the *Ashland*.

The wreck of the *Tasmania* is often buoyed as part of Ontario's Pelee Passage Preserve. Her iron ore cargo lies in a vast pile that has split her hull.

See *Erie Wrecks West* for more information on the *Tasmania*.

The Wisconsin

The steamer *Wisconsin* was relatively lucky in this October storm. She was being towed out of safe harbor at Lorain, Ohio. However, when she was released from the tow, she went on the new east breakwall. The freighter had to anchor outside the harbor all night. In the morning, the tug *Harvey Goulder* brought her into drydock in order to check the 250 feet of her bottom plates suspected of being damaged.

The steamer Wisconsin, at the Lorain breakwater.

Plain Dealer, October 21, 1905.

The Sarah E. Sheldon

The crew of the steamer *Sarah Sheldon* would have been happy had she made the east breakwall at Lorain, Ohio. As it was, at about the time the *Wisconsin* was departing Lorain, the *Sheldon's* superstitious Captain Garant rushed to leave Cleveland on a stormy Thursday evening. This would prevent him from leaving on a "jinxed" Friday sailing day! The *Sheldon* carried a cargo of coal, slated for Sarnia, Ontario. Only a short distance out in the raging storm, the *Sheldon* began to leak as she plowed into the tempest's headwinds. With her thirteen man crew now desperately manning the pumps, Captain Garant made an anxious dash toward Lorain. It was just getting light when Mrs. F.C. Miller, at her "elegantly furnished" summer home in Lake Breeze (Sheffield Lake, Ohio), heard the dying blasts from the *Sarah Sheldon's* whistle. Mrs. Miller telephoned the dock office to report that a big steamer had gone on the rocks about a quarter mile from the resort town.

Sarah E. Sheldon.

Going to the rescue was the tug *Kunkle Brothers*. She set out from Lorain under command of Captain McRae, who had already had a busy day. He and his tug were the ones who had towed the *Wisconsin* out of Lorain and cut her loose, only too see her crash onto the breakwaters. The tug struggled six miles to the wreck site. On arrival, they found that two crewmen had been swept away while trying to launch a leaky lifeboat. Captain Garant directed the tug to first look for Fox and Johansen, the two lost sailors. When a two hour search proved futile, the *Kunkle Brothers* tug returned to the stricken steamer. Captain McRae put the tug perilously close to the rocking steamer and urged the sailors to jump. Only five men complied, in part

SHIP WRECK ON LAKE ERIE, STEAMER SHELDON.

Vintage postcard of the *Sarah Sheldon* aground. Authors' collection.

THINKS LITTLE OF BRAVE DEED

Capt. Motley, With His Men, Takes Lorain Rescue as Matter of Course.

Doesn't Consider His Calling More Risky Than Many Others.

Plain Dealer, October 22, 1905

THOUGHT DEATH AWAITED THEM

Capt. Garant Says Experience Was Worst in 26 Years on Lakes.

Saw Men Float to Destruction and Could Not Help Them.

STAFF SPECIAL.

LORAIN, O., Oct. 20.—"I have been sailing on the lakes for twenty-six years, but today's experience was the toughest thing that I was ever up against," said Capt. Joseph A. Garant of the wrecked steamer Sheldon in an interview today.

Capt. Garant said: "We left Cleveland at 11 o'clock Thursday night in a calm sea. This morning, at about 3 o'clock the wind began to blow a pretty stiff breeze. At 5 o'clock our boat sprung a leak and the water came into the hold in such quantities that our pumps could not keep it down.

"One of the yawl boats had been let down from the davits to be used in an emergency and the sea was so heavy that the boat was filled with

CAPT. JAMES W. GASANT.

Cleveland Plain Dealer article of October 21, 1905.

because they were interested in saving their baggage. By now, both boats had been thrown into such shallow water that Captain McRae decided to return to Lorain.

Fortunately for the remaining crew of the *Sheldon*, the Cleveland Lifesaving Station had also been alerted. The tug *Frank W*, towing a large lifeboat, spent six hours trying to get to the scene. By now, the *Sheldon's* deck was under water, and a crowd had gathered amid the flotsam on the beach. Although every man had cork lifejackets on, they began to grab doors, planks, and anything that would float. The crew did not believe the lifejackets were sufficient to save them.

The tug *Frank W* found the water was too shallow to get near the steamer, so the big surfboat was played out on a line from the tug. Captain Motley, chief of the Cleveland Lifesavers, outlined the crew's rescue effort. According to the *Lorain Times Herald* of November 23, 1905, Captain Motley reported, "I tell you it looked for a time as if someone would have to come out and rescue the lifesavers. The boat was in such a peculiar position that there was no lee side. When an extra big wave would strike up, we would be fifteen feet above the wrecked steamer looking down on her decks."

"If one wave had come sufficiently hard to drop us over on her deck, I am afraid it would have been all up with us. … When we finally did get them off the wreck and into our boat, we put them down in the bottom and threw canvas over them. They were half frozen and faint from exposure."

This storm established the need for a lifesaving station in Lorain. Three years after the incident, Captain Motley and his crew received a Carnegie Lifesaving Metal for their day long battle with this horrendous storm.

Perhaps the *Sheldon's* skipper should have worried less about the Friday sailing jinx and more about the "old superstition that exists among marine men that a cat brings bad luck to a boat" (*Lorain Times Herald* 10/21/1905). Among the timbers that washed ashore at Lake Breeze was the body of a feline. Captain Garant, who had never had an accident in his sailing career, broke down completely over the loss of his two men.

The *Sarah E. Sheldon* lies on a rock bottom off Sheffield Lake. Her shallow remains are widely scattered.

See *Erie Wrecks West* for more information on the *Sheldon*.

The schooner Kingfisher, that went to pieces near the foot of Case ave.

Plain Dealer, October 21, 1905

F.H. Prince

The Kingfisher

The schooner *Kingfisher* was resting aground at the foot of Cleveland, Ohio's Case Avenue. She had been lying there since October 5th, when she was torn from her mooring at the Lakeshore Lumber Dock and washed on the beach east of Cleveland. The October 19 storm would crush this vessel and finish one of her crewmen.

Lake Erie had almost drowned the *Kingfisher's* sailors that terrible night. However, the only crewman lost was her wheelsman, John Fox. He was popular and well known in marine circles. Originally from Port Huron, Fox had lived in Cleveland for many years. After escaping from the stranding of the *Kingfisher*, he went ashore to his boarding house for two weeks. On Wednesday the 18th, he shipped on the ill-fated steamer *Sarah E. Sheldon*. By Friday, Lake Erie had claimed two crewmen from the steamer. John Fox's body was recovered in a fishnet off Fairport, Ohio.

The F. H. Prince

Also fairing badly at Cleveland was the packet boat *F.H. Prince*. When the vessel's crew foolishly left the Cuyahoga River, they learned almost immediately that it was impossible to make headway in the furious storm. With Captain Motley and his lifesavers standing by, she finally regained the harbor. Her cargo had shifted in the battle at the harbor entrance, and she came close to being dashed on the rocks. The *Prince* was later lost at Kelleys Island when she caught fire and was beached in 1911.

See *Erie Wrecks West* for more information on the *Prince*.

The Yukon

The fury of the October 20th storm increased as it raced across the length of the lake. The schooner/barge *Yukon* had been built in 1893. Like the

Tasmania, she was built as a four master. The steamer *F.M. Osborne* entered Lake Erie downbound at the Detroit River just before the storm hit. She was towing the barges *Yukon* and *Gregor*. The *Gregor* was dropped at Huron, Ohio. Though the *Yukon* had a slow leak as she exited the Detroit River, there was little concern until the steamer tow neared Cleveland. The seas at this time were rolling over the *Yukon's* stern and continuously extinguishing the flames in the boiler that powered her pumps. The crew finally had to abandon the boiler room.

Captain Bangs was working on deck when he was overwhelmed by a huge wave that smashed his face into a rail. The *Osborne* and *Yukon* finally made it to Ashtabula, Ohio, where the cargo of the *Yukon* was consigned, on the 20th of October. They dared not enter Ashtabula in the towering seas, so both vessels cast out their anchors approximately two miles off the harbor. Waves continued to roll the length of the barge, and the seven man crew dared not move along her decks. About an hour after she anchored, the *Yukon* started to settle. A distress flag was raised. Seeing the distress flag, the steamer *Osborne* hove anchor and came to their aid. When the steamer tried to maneuver near the barge, both vessels crashed together. One daring sailor from the *Yukon* grabbed a line and was pulled to the *Osborne*. Captain Bangs recognized that the *Osborne* would probably destroy both vessels trying to save his crew. So, he motioned for the *Osborne* to leave.

While the *Osborne* went on to her intended port of Erie, Pennsylvania, the tug *Thomas Wilson* braved the storm to come to the aid of the sinking barge. After five attempts, Captain Tim Haggerty was able to take off the *Yukon's* crew. It was fitting that the tug *Thomas Wilson* was the courageous rescue vessel. The first owner of the *Yukon* was Thomas Wilson of the Wilson Transportation Company.

A sorrowful Captain Lewis Bangs mourned leaving his Newfoundland dog behind on the foundering *Yukon*. But, the constant companion of the captain survived the wreck. When the men left the barge, the

Yukon before she was cut down to a barge. Great Lakes Historical Society photo.

Yukon after she was cut down to a barge. Authors' Collection

dog was perched on the cabin top. When the *Yukon* settled, the dog and cabin were blown twenty-five feet into the sky. This was caused by air in the hold being compressed by the inrushing water. The dog regained the cabin and floated ashore. Captain Bangs learned that his Newfoundland was safe via a telegram.

Shortly after the barge was sunk, she was struck by a steamer. This carried away both of her masts. As she was in line with the harbor entrance and only a mile off, she was cleared by dynamiting in July 1906. Some scattered wreckage from the *Yukon* may still protrude from the bottom off Ashtabula.

The Mautenee and Noguebay

The steamer *Lizzie Madden* set off early in October 1905 with two large barges in tow. Before getting too far from Bayfield, Wisconsin, she lost the barge *Noguebay* to fire and storm. By the end of the voyage, she had lost the second consort, *Mautenee* to the October 19 and 20 blow. Certainly, this was a most unprofitable tow.

Both of the wooden barges carried donkey boilers at the bow. These small boilers provided power to the windlass and to unloading machinery. The *Noguebay* caught fire near the donkey boiler during a storm as she made her way to her homeport of Bay City, Michigan. She was beached and burned to the waterline.

The *Mautenee* ultimately made Buffalo, New York with her lumber cargo. She had not gotten far on the return voyage, when she was severed from her tow. The barge attempted to anchor, but was driven ashore. One crewman swam a line to shore. All of the sailors and the cook, Mrs. Katy Daly, were rescued by breeches buoy.

The loss of the *Mautenee* is detailed elsewhere in this volume.

The Siberia

The crew of the steamer *Siberia* breathed a sigh of relief. The October 19 and 20th storm had almost sent them to the bottom in the deep water off Long Point. Bound to Buffalo with a cargo of barley, she was so roughly treated by the waves that her steam pipes broke. Now unable to work her pumps, she settled so low in the water that her alarmed crew hoisted a distress flag on her foremast. She was observed by the crews of the steamers *H.S. Wilkenson* and *George W. Peevey*. Though both steamers had concerns about their own safety, the lead boat, *Wilkenson*, dropped in behind the ailing *Siberia*. The *Peevey's* crew watched through their marine glass as the convoy trudged through the seas along the Long Point Peninsula. As she neared Long Point Light, the *Wilkenson* left the steamer, and Captain Phillip Smith of the steamer *Wade* took charge. The *Wade* had been sheltering under Long Point. By this time, the *Siberia* had measured eleven feet of water in her hold. Throwing the *Siberia* a line, the *Wade* dragged her under the lee of the point. There, in shallower and calmer water, she settled to the bottom. Captain Smith took off Captain Benham, First Mate W.E. Moore, and the rest of the exhausted *Siberia's* crew and landed them in Buffalo.

For a day or two, the remnants of the Friday storm kept the Gilchrist Fleet from sending pumps to the *Siberia* at her resting place in eighteen feet of water on a sand bottom. By Monday however, the entire crew of the *Siberia* and a steam pump were back aboard the steamer and everyone was confident she would be saved.

The *Siberia* from Great Lakes Historical Society Bowen Collection

Meanwhile, an irate Captain Benham had brought charges against Captain Boyce of the *George W. Peevey*. Captain Boyce made reply in the *Cleveland Plain Dealer* on Thursday, October 26, 1905. While acknowledging he had observed the *Siberia* in distress, he noted that his vessel had a disabled cylinder, and it appeared that the *Wilkenson* had accepted responsibility for the stricken freighter. A vehement Captain Boyce ended his protest by saying, "I have sailed the lakes over forty years and have never deserted a shipmate in time of trouble or refused to render assistance when needed. A man who would do so is not worthy of the name sailor."

The wrecking tug *Saginaw* was working on the *Siberia* a week later when she was forced into Port Rowan by a northeast storm. Now the hull of the *Siberia* was completely at the mercy of the waves. That finished her destruction.

For more information on the *Siberia*, see *Erie Wrecks East* or *Erie Wrecks East, Second Edition*.

Ten sailors from six different vessels lost their lives on Lake Erie in the 1905 storm. Harder hit was Lake Huron where over twenty five casualties were recorded, and the largest wooden schooner ever constructed in Canada, the 245 foot *Minnedosa*, foundered.

The Clarion

To die of fire or ice seemed the fate of six men on the burning package freighter *Clarion*. The *Clarion* was east bound from Chicago to Erie with a cargo of flour, oilcake, and other live stock feed. Her last trip of the season for the Anchor Line was perilously interrupted as she neared the lightship at

The Steamer Clarion.

Pelee Passage. A violent wind from the southwest shook the freighter, igniting something between decks at about 7:00pm on December 8th. As the four men on the nearby lightship *Kewaunee* watched, "compelled by the terror of the scene to look on", the blazing vessel drifted to the west.

Captain Hackett and the rest of the light vessel's crew must have doubted their own ice laden ship would survive. In any case, they had no way to get a boat to the stricken steamer. They did not even know that there were survivors. As it turned out, Captain Hackett gave this account, "Above the thrashing of the waves, the crackling of flames and the noise and confusion all about, the voices of men, crying for help … They must have suffered terribly, as on one side of them they were being scorched and blistered … while on the other side the zero cold water was washing over them" (Sunday, December 12, 1909, *Cleveland Leader*).

The *Clarion's* mate, James Thompson, had gone to check the fire in the hold. He died in the effort. Now Captain James Bell knew that the only possible way to save his men from the furious flames was to launch a yawl and try to make the light

vessel. The captain and twelve others, who had been cut off by the inferno, launched a boat. Six men at the stern watched as it pulled toward the *Kewaunee*. Meanwhile, Chief Engineer A.E. Welcher and five others lowered their yawl and then watched it swamp and drift away. Oiler George McCauley leapt into the sea, trying to make the boat. He succeeded just as a huge wave took him down.

As the chief engineer recounted, "The fire had us hemmed in and there was only one of two things to do. Stay and burn to death or swim for it. They talk of being human. Why, while our ship was all ablaze, a freighter passed so close we could almost read her name. She never stopped, but went right ahead. The fire had now been burning four hours with no signs of abating. We had all given up hope when the steamer *L.C. Hanna* of Cleveland hove in

ICE COVERED LIGHTSHIP HERE
WITH GHASTLY TALE OF WRECK.

This is a view of the Kewaunee, who, powerless to aid, saw the burning of the steamer Clarion. Reading from left to right the men are: William Goslin, mate; F. B. Hackett, captain; Dave Kett, engineer, and Milton Benson, cook.

sight. Captain Anderson saw our plight and, like a good sailor, put about to run along side … The fire at the time the *Hanna* came in sight was dangerously close, and it would only have been a matter of time before we went."

Unbeknownst to the surviving crew of the of the *Clarion* the vessel they thought ignored their plight was the *Josiah G. Monroe*, which fetched up on Southeast Shoal while attempting to rescue them. Captain Sayre of the *Monroe* gave a graphic account in the December 17, 1904, *Cleveland Leader*. According to him, in the heavy sea it was intensely cold and a dense vapor obscured the lower lights of passing ships. Then, his crew heard voices above the roar of the gale. Out of the spray, a steamer appeared only 200 feet off the *Monroe's* bow. As a whistle of distress tore through the howl of the storm, they spotted men with lanterns on the deck.

Captain Sayre ordered his engines worked in reverse, but a perverse wind sent the distressed vessel in another direction. His men vainly tried to get closer to the fire ship, but the helm would not answer. Next, the rescue vessel spotted a huge flare of flame along the middle of the Anchor liner. The *Josiah Monroe* throbbed with the effort to back up as water cascaded over the rails. The *Clarion's* sailors were spotted pulling on the oars with superhuman strength, trying to reach Captain Sayre's vessel. Angry waves tossed the lifeboat away. While this struggle was going on, the *Monroe's* crew saw a man fall from the *Clarion* as a second lifeboat was being launched.

As the crisis continued, the modock whistle on the Southeast Shoal lightship sounded the danger signal. Now, the *Monroe* was in trouble. It had reached the shallows. Captain Sayre again reversed engines, but before they could overcome the force of the wind, the *Monroe* ran aground. Knowing they could no longer help the burning vessel, Captain Sayre reported, "Tears bedimmed the eyes of my gallant men as they still clung to the ice covered railings of the *Monroe* and watched the doomed crew drifting away."

Shortly after leaving the Detroit River at 8:00pm on December 9, Captain Mathew Anderson of the

steamer *Leonard C. Hanna* spied a burning vessel. A sailor's pact to aid another vessel, even at your own peril, sent the *Hanna* through the sleet to the aid of the unknown boat. High on the cabin roof stood six living men with ice covered faces. Captain Anderson said, "As we neared the *Clarion* the first time, I saw the cabin splinter and fall in – a mast fell and flames and sparks shot high in the air. So heavy was the rising steam as the fire and water met, so dense was the overhanging smoke, so vague was one small light circling on the deck, that we couldn't see the wreck. Her siren was blowing

Hanna brings her gunnels against the burning *Clarion*.
Marine Review, January 1910

lustily. Then I knew that we must do good work. We moved around her trying to get in – twice we grazed her bow and the third time as we slid away five of her men jumped across. It took half an hour to get close enough for Welch (the chief engineer)."

"We carried the six men below and gave them stimulant. One had his cheek and his foot frozen.

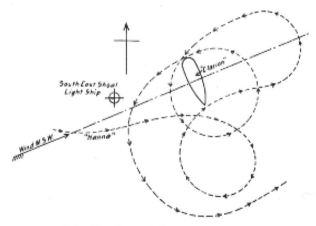

Path of the *Hanna* during the *Clarion* rescue.

Welch had two fingers twisted and frozen. His face was covered with ice. When they had been warmed a little, they cried."

"In the midst of the manipulating, and while the last man was jumping over to us, I heard a voice from the dark on the other side of the wreck. I looked for the boat containing the *Clarion's* captain and twelve men who put off from her – but to find them in that smoke and sea was beyond our power."

Alva B covered in ice.

Six inches of ice coated the tug *Alva B* as she returned with a sleepless crew and hope extinguished that any of the thirteen men in the *Clarion's* lifeboat had survived the brutal storm. The *Alva B* had left Cleveland on a 230 mile, thirty-six hour cruise vainly seeking survivors. When only ten miles out, the door to the bunkroom froze shut, trapping the Alva B's nine man crew in the pilot house. Traveling from Rondeau to Pelee Point and back to Rondeau on the Ontario side had been a fight against the huge seas and biting cold. It was with resigned exhaustion that Captain J.P. Ryan and his brave crew guided the *Alva B* back to the south shore with the sad news that the men on the lifeboat must be at the bottom of Lake Erie. It would be ten months later that the body of the *Clarion's* captain, T.J. Bell was found along the north shore.

The final resting place of the *Clarion* is in deep

water more than ten miles from Southeast Shoal.

See *Erie Wrecks West* for more information on this wreck.

The W.C. Richardson

The *W.C. Richardson* was only seven years old as she neared Buffalo, sliding before the snow flecked gale. Now, only two miles from safety, the *Richardson* impaled herself on Waverly Shoal.

Against Captain Enos Burke's wishes, the number two lifeboat was launched with chief engineer Samuel Mayberry, second mate Sidney Smith and three other crewmen. They were carried off in the frothing seas and lost.

The stern of the *Richardson* started to settle, so at some point, the aft end crew tried to make it to the wheelhouse. It was then that Mrs. John Bradford, wife of the steward, was almost washed overboard. Although the crew sent up rockets, no one ventured out of nearby Buffalo Harbor to help.

Fortunately, Captain Emil Detlefs of the *W.C. Paine* was willing to subject his weary men, on their last voyage of the season, to a daring rescue. The master of the *Paine* had declined to enter Buffalo Harbor because the boat's steering gear had been damaged as she made her way downbound in Lake Erie with an unstable flax

Richardson covered in ice.

W. C. Richardson. Author's collection.

cargo. This was the same cargo carried by the *Richardson*. Now at anchor, Captain Detlefs described the rescue of the remainder of the Richardson's crew in the December 12, *Plain Dealer*,

"It was blowing so hard and the sea was rolling so high that, with the *Paine* disabled, we couldn't go to the *Richardson* that night. We lay to and waited till daylight Thursday morning … On her pilot house, huddled together like sheep, were the men. We couldn't tell how many.

Drawing of the *Paine's* daring rescue of the *W.C. Richardson*. *Marine Review*, January 1910.

We went to her, keeping the *Paine* out of the trough of the sea as best we could. We were dragging one anchor, and when we had drifted near enough to her, we let over the other anchor and kept the engines working all the time. It was pretty careful work, but finally, we got near enough so that the bow of the *Paine* touched that of the *Richardson*. Then we put a ladder over and pulled the men aboard.

The *Richardson* aground on Waverly Shoal

The men were in poor shape. Some of them we had to fasten lines around and pull them over. Others could walk. They were almost frozen and exhausted, as they had no fire nor heat for more than twenty-four hours. … Their clothing was frozen stiff. They were absolutely helpless when we found them and made a happy crowd when we got them aboard the *Paine*."

Cleveland vessel owners and other marine men marveled at the seamanship required to rescue the six men on the *Clarion* and the fourteen men on the *Richardson*. A purse was circulated to collect money for gold watches to present to Captain Anderson and Captain Detlefs, who risked their own crews to rescue suffering sailors. In addition, though the *Paine* had slight damage from the scrape with the *Richardson*,

Charles Spademan

Captain Detlefs was promoted by owner Charles Hutchenson to command the newly launched 524 foot long steamer *A.A. Augustus*.

It was hopped that the *Richardson* could be re-floated, but an icy winter on the shoal finished her off.

For additional information on the *Richardson*, see *Erie Wrecks East, second edition*.

The Charles Spademan

On Friday, December 10, 1909, the steamer *Huron City* departed Huron, Ohio with the thirty-six year old schooner *Spademan* in tow. Though the stormy weather had not abated, they were headed for Marine City, Michigan with cargos of coal. Nearing the Lake Erie Islands, they encountered skim ice that rapidly increased, obstructing their passage. Captain Paul Revard decided to bring the tow about near South Bass Island. A couple of hours of slow going later, the aging *Spademan* was found to have been cut by the ice. Turning back in the storm, the *Huron City* lashed herself to the distressed schooner. Lines were lowered and the cook, Mrs. Struebling, Captain James Bond, and two seamen were hoisted aboard. Ten minutes later, the *Charles Spademan* was on the bottom.

The wooden *Huron City* almost shared the same fate as the *Spaceman's* as she battled her way back to Huron through miles of ice. The steamer's cargo of coal was not delivered until the following spring.

For more on the *Charles Spademan,* see *Erie Wrecks West.*

The Marquette and Bessemer No.2

Captain Robert Rowen McLeod had earned the right to command the carferry *Marquette and Bessemer No.2*. He had been master of four other carferrys, the *Osceola, Colorado,* and *Ann Arbor* on Lake Michigan, and the *Shenango No.1* that traveled between Conneaut, Ohio and Port Stanley, Ontario. His older brother, John, who was former master of the *Shenango No. 1*, which burned at Conneaut in March of 1904, was appointed first mate.

Marquette and Bessemer No.2 Authors' collection

Captain Robert Rowan McLeod

At 10:30am on Tuesday, December 7, 1909, the *M&B #2* slipped out of Conneaut and blew farewell blasts to a crew installing a new fog signal on the breakwall. On the hillside above the harbor, storm signals were whipping in the wind and a light snow was falling. In spite of the ominous weather, Captain McLeod had orders that meant his vessel sailed unless it was blocked by winter ice. The *M&B#2* was loaded with 26 rail cars of coal, one car of castings, three cars of steel and additional structural steel in her belly. The trip across the lake to Port Stanley was almost sixty miles. At her normal cruising speed, the carferry should have docked before the early winter sunset. Then again, this was to be no average stormy day.

On board the ferry was a crew of 31 men and one passenger, Albert Weiss of Erie Pennsylvania. Mr. Weiss, treasurer of Keystone Fish Company, was on his way to Canada to purchase a Canadian fish business. He had arrived late, and the *M&B #2* actually had to return to the dock to pick up their sole passenger. Through the years, unfounded treasure rumors have persisted that he carried $50,000 cash for the purchase of the fish company.

The afternoon of December 7 the *Marquette and Bessemer* No.2 met the 60-foot fish tug *Alberta T.* Captain McLeod, dressed in a southwester and fur coat, attempted to speak to the tug's crew through a megaphone but his words were carried away by the westerly gale. The men on the *Alberta T* thought they heard the word HELP and assumed Captain McLeod was asking if they needed any help. Later that afternoon, a Port Stanley customs

official saw the ship attempting to make it into the harbor. The officer stated that, with the snow and huge waves, it was impossible for the *M&B #2* to enter, and he saw the carferry head west toward Rondeau Harbor. Unknown to Captain McLeod, the experiences of another rail boat, the bulk freighter *Marquette and Bessemer* No.1, indicate that *M&B #2* could not have entered Rondeau Harbor. The *M&B #1* left Conneaut for Rondeau in milder weather six hours before the *M&B #2* left for Port Stanley. She was unable to enter Rondeau and spend over six hours trying to hide from the brutal waves to the east of Rondeau, off Point Aux Pins. Of note, neither Port Stanley nor Rondeau had proper lighting or marine signals.

At 3:10am Wednesday, December 8th, the Port Stanley customs official again thought he heard the ferry's whistle. In conflict with this report, a Mrs. Large, who lived eight miles east of Conneaut, reported seeing the carferry's lights just before

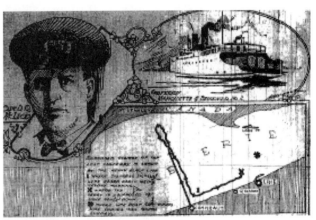

Suspected path of the *M&B #2* was printed in the December 15 *Erie Daily Times.*

midnight on December 7th. Also, William Rice, a Hulett unloader operator at Conneaut Harbor heard distress calls at 1:30am on Wednesday, December 8th. He recognized the calls to be the carferry's horns. Later, an anchor signal was given. This was followed by repeated distress calls.

As days passed, the newspapers were filled with stories of the loss of the *Clarion* and *Richardson.* Meanwhile, the storm had created a new sandbar at Port Burwell. The carferry *Ashtabula*, which plied the waters between Ashtabula, Ohio and Port Burwell on the north shore, plowed into this bar

VICTIMS FOUND IN ICY YAWL BOAT

Commodore Perry's Crew Makes Gruesome Discovery on Lake Erie---Small Craft Tossing on Waves With its Heavy Burden of Stiffened Forms Once Members of Car Ferry's Crew.

Headline from the December 13, *Lorain Daily Times.*

and lay across the mouth of the harbor. It would be two weeks before she was released.

Apprehension for the lost carferry *M&B#2* was increasing, although she had gone to shelter and been missing for up to four days in the past. In fact, a month before, Captain McLeod had tried to prevent flooding in an intense November blow by keeping his boat headed into the wind. However, as the boat

sank into the trough of the seas, water raced inboard and caused the *M&B* to list. One man, working on the coal cars, was swept to the boat's edge by a heavy sea. The *Marquette and Bessemer No.2* had barely survived that passage.

Of that November gale, crewman Jack King of London, Ontario recounted to his friends in a letter that, "The jacks and levers which held the cars on the tracks began to give, and there was much anxiety among the crew. There are four rows of tracks on the boat, and each of these tracks contains eight cars." King went on to tell his friends that, "if the loaded cars on one side

Lifeboat from the *Marquette and Bessemer No.2*

were to go off … the weight of the cars on the other side of the boat would have caused the *M&B* to go over." His friends advised him to give up the job, but his old love of the sea came first.

The *Conneaut News Herald* of Friday, November 19, 1904 declared, "Old seadogs, hardened to every sort of watery peril, declared that it is a practical marvel that, under the conditions as they existed on the boat when she was hardest beset, that Captain McLeod ever brought her into port."

G. LAWRENCE RETURNS AS ONE FROM THE DEAD TO GREET HIS FRIENDS

Was Believed To be Among the Car Ferry Victims ---Missed It By a Fraction of Time On Account Of Meeting His Sweetheart

When George Lawrence showed up after the memorial service, it caused quite a stir.

On Sunday, December 12, the state fisheries commission boat, *Commodore Perry* made a grisly discovery. Captain Driscoll and crew hurried to the aid of a low riding green yawl boat 15 miles north of Erie, Pennsylvania. Nine men were observed sitting in *Lifeboat #4*, but upon hailing the vessel, there was no answer … all nine were frozen. Some of the lifesavers broke down when they saw their silent forms seated in the lifeboat. The *Commodore Perry* took the *Marquette and Bessemer No.2's* lifeboat in tow. By the time they reached Erie, other boats had brought tidings of the disaster, and hundreds of people were gathered at the docks. The frozen crewmen were dressed lightly and some had apparently tried to cover and provide warmth for the

smallest man of the crew, Manuel Souars. Beside the bodies, two knives, a flask, a cleaver, pocketbook, and clothing (possibly worn by a 10th man) were found in the lifeboat.

Three days before the ferry's disappearance, Sarah Clancy, sister of *M&B #2* watchman John Clancy, had a dream of a sinking vessel and her brother's voice. Now it seemed as if her dream was a prophecy. As reports of wreckage and an empty yawl found on the Canadian shore came in, all hope was abandoned for the rest of the sailors aboard the *M&B #2*. Vessel men noted that the *#2* had no stern gates. These were to have been added to the ship before the next season.

Two crewmen of the missing carferry did survive. Max Sparuk, a fireman, was injured and lying in a St. Thomas, Ontario hospital when the ship sailed. Even more remarkable, George Lawrence, the ship's porter, had accidentally left the ferry in Port Stanley the day before her last voyage. He had been sent by engineer Wood to scout for more men when he met his girl. Distracted until he

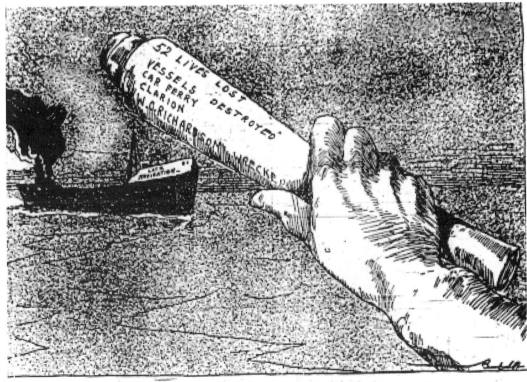

Will this stop it?

Editorial cartoon in the December 12, *Cleveland Leader* called for an end to late season shipping. Finally, too many lives had been lost.

heard the ferry's whistle, he missed her sailing. He alerted a company agent, and assumed everyone knew of his good fortune. When a replacement boat for the *M&B #2* finally arrived from Michigan, he shipped on board. Meanwhile, a memorial service mourning his and the other sailors' deaths had been held some two days before his startling return.

On Sunday, December 20, nearly 900 people crowded the auditorium of the new Conneaut High School. On the stage were a black draped anchor and seven ministers. Conneaut had been devastated by the loss of the *Marquette and Bessemer* No.2. More than half of the 31 crewmembers called Conneaut home. A large number of children had lost their fathers, so a widow's relief fund had already collected $850. In the service, it was noted that 131 sailors had lost their lives on the lakes in 1909. More than half the losses were on Lake Erie and one fourth were from the small town of Conneaut.

On October 5, 1910, ten months after the loss of his ship, the body of Captain Robert Rowan McLeod washed up on Long Point. That same day, the replacement *Marquette and Bessemer* No.2 began her maiden voyage from Cleveland, Ohio. The new vessel had several upgrades, including a wireless, enclosed upper pilot house, and stern gates.

On a gale lashed night in December 1910, there was no port in a storm for the *Marquette and Bessemer* No.2. While rumors often surface that she has been found, the location of this 350-foot steel shipwreck is still a mystery.

See *Erie Wrecks East, 2nd Edition* or *Erie Wrecks West* for additional information on this wreck.

Up until that time, the destruction of the storm of December 8 to 10 of 1909 exceeded all but the losses incurred in the gale of October 20, 1905. The *Plain Dealer* noted that seventy five sailors had been lost on Lake Erie that year. Fifty men had been lost on Lake Superior, six on Lake Michigan and, curiously, none on Lake Huron. A recommendation was made to close the shipping season on December 1st, but it was too late for the 51 men who were buried in foam and ice in early December of 1909.

The new carferry that replaced the *Marquette and Bessemer* No.2. Oddly enough, it was also named *Marquette and Bessemer No.2.*

BLACK FRIDAY

More often than not, when the loss of a vessel is caused by vicious weather, more than one ship is lost. Such was the case on October 20, 1916. The day is commonly known as **Black Friday**, because Lake Erie's most infamous killer storm occurred on that day. Other gales have produced more casualties, but the loss of four large vessels and the dramatic rescues of two captains, who were the sole survivors of their boats, fuel the story that this day saw the worst seas Lake Erie has ever produced.

The Marshall F. Butters

The story began as the wooden lumber hooker *Marshall F. Butters* exited the Detroit River into Lake Erie. Sheltered by Lake Erie's western islands Captain Charles McClure guided the *Butters* safely past the Southeast Shoal light. The realization that this was not an ordinary blow probably dawned on the captain a short while later when the aging 164 foot long ship began to roll heavily shifting the cargo of lumber and shingles piled high on

Marshall F. Butters

her deck. While the captain changed course for Lorain Harbor, the fourteen man crew struggled mightily to trim the ship. However angry waters soon put out her fires. As she was pushed before winds estimated

Lumber litters the lake as the *Marshall F. Butters* founders.
Great Lakes Historical Society photo

at seventy miles per hour, Captain McClure repeatedly sounded her whistle with the rapidly diminishing steam.

Though nothing could be heard over the shriek of the wind, two vessels had noted telltale puffs of steam from the doomed *Butters*. Eleven sailors perilously launched a lifeboat as the freighters *Frank R. Billings* and *F.G. Hartwell* struggled to the scene. Captain F.B. Cody of the *Billings* soon lost sight of the *Hartwell* and the first lifeboat, but kept an eye on three silhouettes waving wildly at the stern of the *Butters*. As he approached the steamer through masses of now floating timber, he ordered his men to put out storm oil to calm the waves. Neil Harrington, wheelsman, Henry Rantz, fireman and Joseph Scheffenger were the last to leave the foundering lumber hooker but became the first ashore when the *Billings* arrived in Cleveland. The men spent many anxious hours waiting word of their shipmates since the snow had obscured the rescue of the first lifeboat's crew, and the *Hartwell* could not safely enter Fairport Harbor for a day.

See *Erie Wrecks West* for additional information on the *Marshall Butters*.

Captain Mattison of the *D.L. Filer*

The D.L. Filer

The schooner barge *D.L. Filer* of Chicago and the barge *Interlaken* were being towed west in worsening weather by the steam barge *Tempest*. As was the custom of the time, when a steamer ran into trouble the tows were cut loose. The two boats were released near Bar Point. The wooden coal barge was a prime candidate for destruction as she was now forty-five years old. Weathered seams opened as water rushed over her decks. As she started to settle in the shallow west end of Lake Erie, Captain Mattison climbed the aft mast, while his crew took to the foremast. Much to the survivors dismay, the howling wind and weight of the six crewmen soon caused the foremast to fall. Only one of the six men was able to swim the 100 or so feet to the after mast to join the captain. Weakened by

D.L. Filer Authors' collection

Merida   Authors' collection

his dip in the chilly waters, crewman Oscar Johansen lost his grip and drowned just as the D & C Liner *Western States'* yawl approached. Captain Mattison spent the next several days near Bar Point searching for the bodies of his lost crew.

See *Erie Wrecks West* for additional information on the *D.L. Filer.*

The Merida

When the newspapers on Sunday October 22nd, 1916 reported the loss of two vessels and six men they were sadly unaware of the storm's true toll. Two wooden boats had succumbed to "Black Friday" but two larger steel ships were, at the time, unknown victims.

Captain Cody of the steamer *Frank R. Billings* had followed the 376-foot long *Merida* out of the Detroit River, and was soon occupied rescuing three men from the hapless *Marshall F. Butters.* The *Billings* and the steamer *Briton* were perhaps the last to see the *Merida.*

Captain J.F. Massey of the *Briton* noted the ore carrier late Friday morning rolling heavily and shipping seas. Captain Harry Jones, mate Gideon Fleming, chief engineer Joseph O'Connor and 20 crew disappeared without a trace sometime that

Captain Grashaw of the *Colgate*
Plain Dealer photo

brutal afternoon. Captain Massey's ship also began taking huge waves over the stern so the *Briton's* captain turned back to shelter at Cedar Point, but not before a tremendous sea demolished the engine room skylight.

Additional information on this wreck is in *Erie Wrecks West*.

The James B. Colgate

Also struggling on "Black Friday" was the whaleback steamer *James B. Colgate* with 40-year-old Captain Walter Grashaw only two weeks into his first command. Lone survivor Captain Grashaw who drifted for an incredible 36 hours on a raft best tells the *Colgate's* loss:

> *"As night came the wind blew harder…we estimated the gale to be blowing at a 74 mile gait. We gathered aft and every man had confidence that we would outride the gale.*

> *After eight o'clock the boat began to list, and we saw something was wrong for'ard. Soon we realized that we were taking water, and it was not long before we were in a mighty bad way.*

> *Some of the men prayed on bended knee. I*

thought of my family and feared for them. One fellow kept speaking about his little ones and another thought only of his mother. All were brave however, and did whatever I asked them to do.

I went to the bridge and turned on the searchlight hoping to attract attention. With the searchlight on I tried to see what was the matter with us. At every plunge and every wave I could see the hatch covers raise and lower as the water in the hold swept for'ard and back.

Finally we went down.

As we felt her giving way we jumped into the water. We had made the boats and life rafts ready. All had put on life preservers…..I suppose they'll carry the bodies of my poor men where they will be found in a few days.

I went over with one of the life rafts. It tossed horribly. When it finally righted itself there were two of the men on it with me, one a man I could not remember having seen before and Harvey Ossman, second engineer.

Not the least sign of wreckage was visible…..

The water was awfully cold. We were

James B. Colgate

drenched of course and the wind seemed to be blowing ice into our skins. All three of us were pretty busy trying to keep on that tossing raft. The raft was only about 5 by 9 feet and we could not move around any. At some point we rolled, and the one fellow was gone. Afterwards Ossman and I battled it out alone the rest of the night. All the time the wind kept driving the water into our hides. I didn't have the least idea that we would ever see daylight.

It was just about getting daylight and the raft went over again. Somehow or other I managed to grab the raft as I came to the surface. I had a mind to let go and quit right there, but something kept me going. I couldn't pull myself out of the water. Suddenly something hit my legs. There was Ossman. He had come up under the raft. I grabbed him by the collar and helped him get hold. I pulled myself further and further and would then turn and help Ossman. He got pretty well up on the raft. Suddenly Ossman gave a cry, tossed his arms and went down.

Left alone I had a time of it staying on the raft. Lying flat on my stomach in the center of the raft I'd kick my legs but could not warm them up. When the raft seemed to be floating pretty well I'd roll over and pound my chest. I can't tell you how long the day seemed.

The sea was going down and I had a few minutes of hope. Then it began to get darker. I can't tell you of the dread and fear of seeing night come again.

Captain Grashaw's family: wife Flora, eldest son Nelson, younger son Walter, Jr., and daughter Marjorie.

At dawn I saw the Buffalo boat. Two puffs of steam indicated I had been seen. Then suddenly the boat steamed by. I cursed the heartless captain." (Conneaut *News Herald*, October 28, 1916)

Rescue was at hand for Captain Grashaw, since close by wheelsman Henderson of the carferry *Marquette and Bessemer* No.2 had also spotted Walter kneeling on a sliver of hope.

Calling his captain, who was getting his first sleep in two days, the ferry put about and grappled the semi-conscious Captain Grashaw to the carferry deck.

When the *Colgate's* captain revived in a Conneaut hospital he first asked if his wife had been notified of his rescue. A grateful Flora Grashaw had already left her three small children and was en route to Grace hospital. This brush with death did not discourage Captain Grashaw who went on to command another whaleback steamer, *Progress*. Ironically he died 12 years later from typhoid contracted after a piece of coal flew off a conveyor belt and cut his lip.

But in the interim, seven-year-old Nelson, 3-year-old Walter junior and baby Marjorie would have a chance to know their father.

While Grashaw was in the hospital, fears for the *Merida* were confirmed with the recovery of six bodies wearing *Merida* lifejackets. Black Friday's toll was four large vessels and fifty lives, including twenty-one sailors from Grashaw's whaleback steamer.

A Captain's Lament

by Georgann Wachter

We left Detroit River and passed Pigeon Bay.
Hugh waves began building, the sky was dark gray.
The boats they did labor as we tested the seas.
Wild wind was a howling, it started to freeze.
I look in the shallows, I scan Erie's shore.
I won't give up searching, till there are no more.

They called it Black Friday, but we couldn't know
The fury that faced us was no average blow.
My men all courageous did all that was asked.
They rushed to the pumps and bent to the task.
I look in the shallows and follow the shore.
I won't give up searching till there are no more.

Black Friday was vicious.
It took my poor men.
A captain's sad duty to gather again.
The sons and the fathers whose love has been lost.
From the Colgate and Filer at a terrible cost.
I look to the beaches, and follow the shore.
The gulls circling round tell me there are more.

If I'd skippered the Butters where they were all saved.
Or like Jones on Merida I'd gone to my grave.
I wouldn't have nightmares of hands reaching out.
As the wind cut right through me, and I heard them shout
For their captain to save them, their children to know,
That they couldn't escape from Black Fridays cruel blow.
So I walk in the shallows and follow the shore.
And I won't give up searching till there are no more.

LIGHTHOUSES OF LAKE ERIE

The "old" Huron Harbor Lighthouse greets steamers entering the harbor.
Photo from Great Lakes Historical Society

The first lighthouse on the Great Lakes was built in 1781 at Fort Niagara by the English government during the Revolutionary War. They had lost the *HMS Ontario*, over 80 military personnel, and a large supply of war provisions in an October 1780 storm. The United States got involved in lighthouse building and maintenance on August 7, 1789 when the 8th bill passed by the fledgling first congress provided that, "All expenses … in the necessary support, maintenance and repair of all lighthouses … shall be defrayed out of the Treasury of the United States."

Lake Erie has the distinction of being home to the first lighthouses built on the Great Lakes by the United States government. The first American lighthouses were necessitated by the country's expansion westward. They were built in 1818 at Buffalo, New York and Erie, Pennsylvania. Both were illuminated for the first time in 1819. Since that time, for nearly two centuries, Lake Erie lighthouses have guided ships on their passages to and through the harbors of the north coast of the United States and the south coast of Canada. The oldest of these is the Buffalo Main Light. Like many of her sisters, this light stands today in near perfect repair. Many others have burned, been torn down, or permitted to decay into ruins. Fortunately, some of

THE LIGHTHOUSE KEEPER WONDERS

The light I've attended for 40 years
is now to be run by a set of gears.
The Keeper said, And it isn't nice
To be put ashore by a mere device.
Now, fair or foul the winds that blow
Or smooth or rough the sea below,
It is all the same. The ships at
night will run to an automatic light.

That clock and gear which truly turn
Are timed and set so the light shall burn.
But did ever an automatic thing
set plants about in early Spring?
And did ever a bit of wire and gear
A cry for help in the darkness hear?
Or welcome callers and show them through
The lighthouse rooms as I used to do?

'Tis not in malice these things I say
All men must bow to the newer way.
But it's strange for a lighthouse man like me
After forty years on shore to be.
And I wonder now--Will the grass stay green?
Will the brass stay bright and the windows clean?
And will ever that automatic thing
Plant marigolds in the early Spring?

Edgar Guest
August 20, 1881 – August 5, 1959

these gracious structures have been restored and still stand along our shores. Some welcome visitors with museums and visitors' centers. Even those in ruins are still picturesque, providing inspiration, and igniting the imagination

Were it not for these beacons in the night, many more ships would have met their fate on the bottom of Lake Erie. This is part of their allure. The stories of daring rescue surrounding many lights is better than any fiction we could write. Yet that is not the only draw of the lighthouse. They are often located at remote and scenic sites. They provide fabulous views of the waters they protect. And, like moths to a light, the human spirit is drawn to the nostalgia and architecture of these Erie lights.

ASHTABULA LIGHTHOUSE

Type: Integral, square, steel and concrete **Established:** 1905 **Status:** Active aid to navigation
Location: Ashtabula, Ohio at north end of west breakwater
GPS: 41 55.114   80 47.756
Access: The light is not accessible by land. It is easily viewed by boat out of the Ashtabula River.
Fast Facts: The Ashtabula Lighthouse light tower stands 40 feet above the lake. Constructed of steel and iron plate, the light was moved to its present location in 1916, and automated in 1973. As of this writing, this site is an operational facility administered by the U.S. Coast Guard and so is not open to the public. However, the Ashtabula Lighthouse Preservation Society has filed their second application to the General Services Administration for ownership of the light.

Ashtabula Lighthouse

Photo by Authors

Story of the Light:

The Ashtabula Lighthouse has the distinction of being the last manned light on Lake Erie. The first lighthouse to grace Ashtabula's shore was built in 1836. It was a hexagonal tower atop a 40-foot-square wooden crib. A wooden ramp connected the tower to the river's east pier. This original light used seven sperm oil lamps to light the night skies.

By 1876 the construction of new dock facilities warranted a new lighthouse. This tower was built on the west pier. It served the harbor for forty years and was upgraded with a fourth order Fresnel lens, a fixed red light, and a siren fog signal in 1896.

The lighthouse that guards Ashtabula today was erected in 1905. At this time the Ashtabula River was widened and a break wall was constructed to provide protection for the harbor.   The current light was originally located 2,500 feet north of the river entrance. Standing 40 feet high, the light is built with steel and iron. Interestingly, the 1876 light house was left standing in the middle of the now widened river. The iron and steel lighthouse was moved to its current location in 1916, one year after construction of an extension of the east breakwater. In order to support the light keeper in the lighthouse, instead of a remote house, the lighthouse structure was doubled in size. Its massive two stories of steel and iron required a 50-foot concrete crib to support it. A new fourth order Fresnel lens was installed, and a radio beacon tower was built next to the lighthouse.

The years 1927 and 1928 held great excitement for the Ashtabula Light. There is an old joke about two marine captains heading for an imminent collision where one says "I am an aircraft carrier, you'll have to get out of my way." The other replies, "I fear you'll have to alter course -- I am a lighthouse." Perhaps this story originated when the Canadian Steamship Lines steamer *Gleneagles* rammed into

the lighthouse in 1927 and drove it six inches back on its foundation. Although the ship sustained major damage, no one was hurt in the lighthouse or on the ship. In 1928, two keepers were in the lighthouse when a huge storm blew in. The storm encased the lighthouse in five foot thick heavy layers of ice. The two keepers were trapped inside for two days before they were able to thaw the door open and tunnel through the five feet of ice.

Another fourth order Fresnel lens and a foghorn, were installed in 1959. The rotating Fresnel lens produced a white flash visible for 19 miles when the night skies were clear. The new beacon was electric and required no operator. However, the foghorn needed to be manned. As a result, the Coast Guard continued to man the Ashtabula Lighthouse until it was fully automated in 1973. At that time, it was the last remaining manned light on Lake Erie.

The original 1836 Ashtabula Lighthouse.
Photo from authors' collection

BARCELONA LIGHTHOUSE

Type: Conical stone   **Established:** 1829   **Status:** Inactive, private residence

Location: Barcelona, New York , one block east of Route 394 on New York Route 5

GPS: 42 20.462   79 35.689

Access: The light is viewable from the right-of-way on Route 5 in Barcelona, or from the pier of the marina immediately to the east of the light. Please respect that it is private property.

Fast Facts: Completed in May 1829. Local boulders and stones were used to construct the tower. It was initially oil lit, but was converted to gas in 1831. It is believed to be the first light in the nation o be powered by natural gas. The light was decommissioned in 1859 because Barcelona didn't actually have a harbor. Today the light is privately owned and is frequently lit by a gas lamp maintained by its owner and the town of Westfield.

Barcelona Lighthouse

Photo by Authors

Story of the Light:

In a town once known as Portland, New York stands a light once known as the Portland Lighthouse. The lighthouse was authorized by the United States Congress on May 23, 1828 after locals had conducted an extensive lobbying campaign. With the opening of the Erie Canal on October 26, 1825, Portland locals were anxious to attract vessel traffic to their small town. Unbeknownst to the U.S. Congress, the town of Portland had no harbor. For 30 years this beacon shone in the night, attracting vessels to the shores near the town of Portland. The community had tried to construct a harbor but the development of the railroads eliminated any real financial opportunity. Finally, in 1859, the Lighthouse Board realized there was no harbor and decommissioned the light.

While all of this was going on, the town of Portland merged into what is now the village of Westfield, New York. A small area surrounding the lighthouse became the hamlet of Barcelona, and the light became known as the Barcelona Light. The hamlet's light has several unique distinctions. It is the only known light to have been authorized and built where there was no harbor or navigational need. It is the first light on the Great Lakes and the first public building in the U.S. to be lighted by natural gas. In addition, the conical fieldstone tower and attached fieldstone dwelling are one of the oldest structures of its kind on the Great Lakes.

The original beacon was made up of eleven patent lamps, each with a 14-inch reflector. There were also two spare lamps. The Barcelona Light was initially equipped with two tin oil tanks housing 500 gallons of oil. History was made on January 1, 1831, when a contract was let to fire the light with natural gas, "at all times and seasons". This made the Barcelona Light the first (and perhaps only) light in the nation to be lit by natural gas. The Portland Harbor (Barcelona) Light and buildings were sold by auction in 1872. In 2005 it was listed for sale on e-bay.

Converting the lighthouse to gas was no easy feat. Early settlers in the area were aware of a flammable gas that constantly issued from fissures in the rocks, which formed the bed of a small stream that flowed into Lake Erie near the lighthouse. They called it the "burning spring." In order to bring the gas from the stream to the lighthouse, a well was dug into the rock and a cone of solid mason work was erected to

contain the gas that would collect in the well. A pipe was inserted at the base of the cone and extended to the lighthouse, making it the first gas well! Next, lamps had to adapted to receive and burn the gas. Since gas lamps had not yet been invented, an area blacksmith, Mr. Hart, designed the lamps. They consisted of several horizontal arms placed like the radii of a semicircle. Each had a brass pipe attached, and the flow of gas was regulated with a stopcock. A reflector was attached behind each burner. Two tiers of these lamps, seven on the bottom and six on the top, made it so the tower provided one unwavering light when viewed from the lake.

The light's first keeper was a deaf clergyman named Joshua Lane. Appointed on May 27, 1829, he was paid a whopping salary of $350 per year to support himself and his *"numerous female dependents"*.

Today, the lantern and light have been removed and replaced with a wood frame that defines where the lantern once was. The current owner still keeps a gas light lit in the tower to remind one and all of the first gas lighted public building in the United States.

When viewed from the recreational harbor, the light tower obscures the keeper's house. Photo by authors.

BUFFALO MAIN LIGHTHOUSE

Type: Octagonal limestone   **Established:** 1833   **Status:** Inactive

Location: Buffalo, New York , at the mouth of the Buffalo River

GPS: 42 52.670   78 53.369

Access: Take the New York Route 5 "Skyway" exit at Fuhrmann Boulevard and follow the signs leading to the Coast Guard Station. The light is located adjacent to the station property and is part of an outdoor museum.

Fast Facts: The original light at this location was a beacon constructed in 1818. This light and the Erie Land Light were the first U.S. lighthouses on the Great Lakes. Because it was too dim, the 1818 light was replaced by the existing tower in 1833. Today it is a landmark and one of the Great Lakes great treasures.

Buffalo Main Lighthouse

Note the "Bottle Light" to the right of the picture. Photo by Authors

Story of the Light:

Since the first light in 1818, the entrance to Buffalo Harbor has been marked by nine different lights and a lightship. Funding for a light was provided by the U.S. Congress in 1805. However, construction was delayed by local politics (nothing ever really changes!). Then came the War of 1812, and Buffalo was burned by the British, interfering with the building of a lighthouse. The original Buffalo Main Lighthouse was finally completed 1818. It shared the honor of being the first U.S. Government Lighthouse on the Great Lakes with the Erie Land Light, both being lit in 1819.   The tower was 30 feet tall, but had something of a weak light. Its reputation for being dim was reinforced when the first steam powered vessel on the lakes above Niagara Falls, the *Walk-in-the-Water*, was coming into port, and the captain could not see the light through the thick smoke of Buffalo resident's wood burning stoves. The ship missed the entrance and ran aground near the light.

With the opening of the Erie Canal in 1925, there was increased vessel traffic, and intensified local claims that the original light was too low and too faint. The decision was made to replace the 1818 light with the structure that stands today. The new Buffalo Main Harbor Light first shone in 1833, and the eighty-foot tower was operational until 1914. The octagonal carved Queenston limestone tower overlooked the terminus of the Erie Canal. This original tower received a third order Fresnel lens in 1856, and the tower was raised three feet in 1905. This made the focal plane 76 feet above lake level. Today, it is the oldest structure in the city of Buffalo. The light sits on a 689 foot octagonal base with a circular stone stairway. The watch room has deeply recessed windows. The tower is capped by an 8-sided iron lantern room.

A third light was built at the end of a 4,000 foot breakwater in the harbor in 1872. This original Buffalo Breakwater Light was a large house-like structure with a fourth order Fresnel lens. Apparently not accustomed to such a bright beacon, ships began using it for target practice. Ships rammed the tower in 1899, 1900, 1909, and 1910, finally forcing it to be rebuilt in 1913. Then, in 1958, the freighter *Frontenac* rammed the Breakwater Light, knocking it back 20 feet and tilting it 15 degrees. As a result, it was called the "leaning light-house", until it was replaced by a new white, seventy-one foot tower in 1961. Two unique Bottle Lights were installed at the ends of additional breakwaters in 1903. These white, cast-iron towers would remain in service until 1985. One can still be viewed next to the Buffalo Main Light. The other is on display at the Dunkirk, New York Lighthouse and Maritime Museum. Also established in 1903 was the South Buffalo Light. It was automated in 1935.

Lightship No. 82 was stationed at the entrance of Buffalo Harbor from 1912 to 1913. The ship and her six man crew were lost in the great storm of November 1913. It was raised, and continued to serve on the Great Lakes for another twenty-three years. *Lightship 82* was the second lightship in the Lighthouse Service's history to sink on station, and the first to go down with the loss of all hands. Only one body was ever found.

Several additional markers have lit the area over time. The Black Rock Range Lights marked the south entrance of the Niagara River from 1853 to 1870. There was a fifth order Fresnel lens in the short rectangular pier lighthouse. The Horseshoe Reef Light of 1856 was in Canadian waters, and required cooperation of the American, Canadian, and British governments. It marked a dangerous point outside Buffalo Harbor. In 1920, the new Buffalo water intake crib had a light built on top of it. This light and the construction of a protected channel to the harbor made the Horseshoe Reef Light unnecessary, and it was abandoned.

Public protest saved Buffalo Main Light when it was scheduled for demolition in the 1960's. fortunately the light was saved and is now leased to Buffalo

Vintage picture of the Buffalo Main Lighthouse from the U.S. Coast Guard

Lighthouse Association, Inc. In 1985, the association restored to the light and installed a Fresnel lens, which is lit for special occasions. Additional repairs were made in 2005.

CEDAR POINT LIGHTHOUSE

Type: Wood tower on stone keeper's house **Established:** 1839 **Status:** Inactive

Location: On the grounds of Cedar Point Amusement Park, Sandusky, Ohio

GPS: 41 29.272   82 41.613

Access: The light is accessible by land in the Cedar Point Amusement Park. It is viewable by boat and from the Lighthouse Point residential area of the park.

Fast Facts: This is the oldest building on Cedar Point. In 1853, a front range beacon was added about 265 feet north of the lighthouse. The lighthouse served as the rear range light for 51 years. In 1910, the front light was destroyed by fire and the tower was removed. The keeper's house continued to be used by the Lighthouse Service and Coast Guard until 1975. It was acquired by the Cedar Point Amusement Park circa 1990. The park renovated the building and rebuilt the tower in 2000-2001. It is now the focal point of the park's Lighthouse Point camping and lodging area.

Cedar Point Lighthouse

Photo by the authors

Story of the Light:

Ask anyone who is familiar with the south shore of Lake Erie about Cedar Point, and they will tell you about Cedar Point Amusement Park. Today, it is the number one rated amusement park in the world, and the second oldest amusement park in North America. Reading the park's official history, we learn that it was established in 1870 as a public bathing beach. The first people arrived at Cedar Point Resort on the steamer, *Young Reindeer*. The first roller coaster on "America's Roller Coast" was not established

The Sandusky Pierhead Light, with Cedar Point Amusement Park in the background, now marks the entrance to Sandusky Bay.

By March 31, 1904, channel improvements and better-placed range lights leading into Sandusky Harbor made the Cedar Point range lights obsolete. Both range lights were discontinued. The Lighthouse Service and later the Coast Guard continued to use the site as a buoy depot, a radio beacon station, and a search and rescue boat station. The light tower was removed from the roof of the main dwelling. The front light was destroyed by fire on July 5, 1910. A large brick duplex was built in the 1920's to house the families of the commander and executive officers of the Coast Guard, while the old lighthouse was used as quarters and galley for enlisted personnel. The boat station was finally closed in 1975 and duties were transferred to the Marblehead Coast Guard Station.

The lighthouse and the property around it were acquired by the Cedar Point Amusement Park around 1990. Fortunately, the park recognized the value of preserving the historic light and had the good sense not to tear it down. In 2000-2001, Cedar Point completely renovated the keeper's

until 1892. Named the Switchback Railway, it stood an incredible 25 feet tall and reached a heart-pounding top speed of 10 m.p.h.. The park will tell you the only thing a visitor from 1870 would recognize today is the beautiful sand beach that graces Cedar Point's coastline. But, thanks in large part to the developers of Cedar Point Amusement Park, that statement is not entirely true. That visitor would also recognize the lighthouse at Cedar Point.

Long before there was an amusement park or a bathing beach, Cedar Point was home to the Cedar Point Light. The original light (a rectangular, stuccoed, stone dwelling) stood only 28 feet tall and was decorated with sawtooth Dutch gables. Established in 1839 to mark the eastern approach to Sandusky Bay, the Cedar Point Light complemented the existing light at the western edge of the bay, Marblehead Light, which went into service in 1821. A front range beacon was added about 265 feet north of the lighthouse in 1853, and Cedar Point Light then served as the rear light of the range. The light was completely rebuilt in 1867 to provide a six room keeper's house made of cut limestone with a short octagonal light tower centered on the roof peak. At 38 feet, the Cedar Point Light was now 10 feet higher.

Roller coasters surround the Lighthouse on the grounds of Cedar Point Amusement Park. Photo by the authors.

house, replaced the light tower and beacon on top and made it the focal point of what is now Lighthouse Point. Lighthouse Point features 64 cottages, 40 cabins and 97 luxury recreational vehicle campsites.

OLD CLEVELAND MAIN LIGHT

Type: Victorian tower   **Established:** 1838   **Status:** Demolished

Location: This light once stood on the east bank of the Cuyahoga River near the Main Avenue Bridge.

GPS: Gdansk Poland replica at 54 24 28   18 39 50

Access: Only through the hearts and dreams of lighthouse enthusiasts.

Fast Facts: Once considered the most beautiful lighthouse in America, a near exact replica of the Old Cleveland Main Light still stands in Gdansk, Poland.

Old Cleveland Main Light

Photo from Great Lakes Historical Society

Story of the Light:

The first Cleveland Main Lighthouse was built by Levi Johnson on a bluff at the north end of Water Street (now W. 9th Street). This light served the city well until, decades later; a tall, Victorian Gothic light was built on the same site in 1873. The story of this light reminds us all of the need to preserve and cherish these beautiful structures.

One look at a picture of this light and your imagination runs wild. Walt Disney could not have envisioned a more striking structure. However, one need not imagine fairytale scenes and heroes. This fabulous tower was home to real heroes, the keepers of the lights. Regrettably, the Old Cleveland Light Station was closed in 1892. Her light had become increasingly difficult for mariners to distinguish from the ever increasing lights of the City of Cleveland. In 1882, officials replaced the mineral-oil lamps in the main light with gas, in a futile effort to increase the beacon's usefulness. Finally, the U.S. Government Lighthouse Board determined that pier lights would be a more effective way to direct mariners into the harbor.

For the next four years, this graceful lady was the victim of neglect. Then a fire in the Cleveland warehouse district did additional damage to the structure and it was vacated in 1896. Some years later, the lighthouse was sold to the Cuyahoga County Commissioners. Some efforts were made to save the unique lighthouse, but the sentinel that had once watched over Cleveland now had no one to look after it. Considered to be beyond repair, the station was dismantled around 1900, and Cleveland's spire was lost forever.

After the beacon was decommissioned, many of the pieces were sent to the Braddock Point Lighthouse on Lake Ontario, which was built in 1892. More importantly, the lighthouse at Gdansk, Poland was modeled after the Old Cleveland Main Light. It seems that visitors from Gdansk came to Cleveland during the 1893 Chicago World Exposition. Struck by the beauty of Cleveland's Victorian lighthouse, they built a full scale copy of it in Gdansk called the Nowy Port Lighthouse. It was from this tower that the opening shots of World War II were fired. On September 1, 1939, at 4:45am German army machine gunners opened fire from its embrasures on the Polish army outpost of Westerplatte, across the Vistula River. At the same time the German Battleship *Schleswig-Holstein* fired a broadside against the Polish outpost. Thus, the Old Cleveland Light played a small part in the beginning of World War II, a war that claimed 55 million lives.

Decommissioned in 1984, the Gdansk Nowy Port Lighthouse reopened in 2004 as a historical monument. It offers visitors a chance to admire its unique architecture and provides an unsurpassed view of the surrounding area. It also offers the opportunity to see what Cleveland lost, an architectural treasure of a lighthouse.

There are lessons to be learned from this experience. The City of Cleveland is now watching history repeat itself. The Old Cleveland Coast Guard Station at the mouth of the Cuyahoga River has stood abandoned and neglected for several years. The city now owns the property and has said it intends to restore it. However, little seems to be happening in that direction. Sound familiar? Perhaps Gdansk will build us a copy of the Coast Guard Station too.

Historic Gdansk Nowy Port Lighthouse.
Photo: B. Nieznalski, www.lighthouse.pl

CLEVELAND PIERHEAD LIGHTS

Type: Conical cast iron towers, black and red lantern **Established:** 1911 **Status:** Active

Location: On the east and west Cleveland Harbor breakwater at the main harbor entrance.

GPS: west light: 41 30.541 81 43.065 east light: 41 30.613 81 42.927

Access: The lights are not accessible by land. They are best seen by boat. Several river cruise boats go by the lighthouses, including the *Goodtime III*, *Holiday* and *Nautica Queen*.

Fast Facts: The sixty-seven foot tall west structure was first lit in 1911. The attached fog signal building was constructed in 1910.

Cleveland West Pierhead Light

Photo by the authors

Story of the Light:

The entrance to Cleveland Harbor and the Cuyahoga River is watched over by lights on two pierheads marking the channel. These lights are actually the third in a series of lights and lifesaving stations built on either side of the Cuyahoga.

The modern history of the crooked river that runs through Cleveland, Ohio began when an 18th century surveyor named Moses Cleaveland was charged with exploring the Connecticut Western Reserve. He arrived at the mouth of the Cuyahoga River in 1796, and began a settlement which became Cleveland, Ohio. Long before Moses arrived, native Mohawk Indians had christened the river Cuyahoga, their word for crooked river. Cleveland remained a small settlement until the Ohio Canal began in 1825. By 1832 the canal extended as far as Portsmouth on the Ohio River. Being the terminus of the Ohio Canal was the impetus for Cleveland's growth. It not only spurred ever increasing trade, but also facilitated the growth of the Cleveland iron foundries, which were first established in 1828. In 1852, two steel companies were established on the river, one at Whiskey Island near the mouth of the river and one up river around collision bend. The next year the waterfront was first used as a harbor. In 1854, 2,544 tons of ore arrived in Cleveland from the Marquette Range.

As commerce grew, piers were constructed along both banks of the Cuyahoga. The original lights were placed on the outermost ends of these piers. Breakwaters were eventually added to provide a protected shipping harbor. The design of the Cleveland breakwaters included a gap aligned with the mouth of the river to permit easy vessel access. Each side of this gap was marked by a light. Finally, in 1910 a pair of spurs was built into the lake extending the entrance of the harbor further into Lake Erie. In 1911, the Cleveland Harbor West Pierhead Lighthouse, the large structure that remains standing today, was built at the eastern end of the extended western breakwater.

Cleveland East Pierhead Light
U.S, Coast Guard

The light consisted of a conical, cast-iron tower that integrated the keeper's quarters. The lantern had a fourth order Fresnel lens. Five years later, in 1916, a fog signal building was added. It put forth a very deep mooing sound that could be heard twelve miles out in the lake. Because it sounded a great deal like a cow, the fog signal was commonly called "the cow".

The lighthouse was automated in 1965. In 1995 the Fresnel lens was donated to the Great Lakes Science Center located on the Cleveland waterfront. It is still on display.

On the opposite side of the harbor entrance is the East Pierhead light. Two lights were considered necessary to help vessels safely navigate between the breakwater arms. The east entrance light was also built in 1911.

After several decades, it was replaced by a modern steel tower. The current cylindrical 47-foot tower is white with a black lantern room. An active aid to navigation, it has a red light that flashes three seconds on, three seconds off.

The tall ship *New Providence*, bracketed by the Cleveland Pierhead Lights
Photo by authors

CONNEAUT LIGHT

Type: Steel cylindrical tower on a square base   **Established:** 1921   **Status:** Active

Location: On end of the west breakwater at Conneaut Harbor, Ohio.

GPS: 41 58.806   80 33.436

Access: The light is not accessible by land. It is best viewed by boat or from the municipal pier of Marina Drive in Conneaut.

Fast Facts: The Conneaut Light is identical to the Huron, Ohio light, which was built the same year. Both were designed to be a break with the past, and represent modern times.

Conneaut Light

Photo by the authors

Story of the Light:

The sleek, modern tower that looks over Conneaut Harbor may not have the "character" of many of the more glamorous lights on the Great Lakes, but it is on the National Register of Historic Places. The registry designation did not come about because of the marvelous old lighthouses that preceded this structure. Rather, it was granted because the design represented a departure from the past. According to

National Register petition reviewer Patrick Andrews, "In the 1930s there was a conscious effort to represent the machine age, speed and efficiency. The style of this lighthouse is a clear attempt to look modern and to make a break from the past."

Like its "sister" spire in Huron, Ohio, the Conneaut Lighthouse is an operational 60-foot steel tower. Before it was automated, the keeper's quarters and supply areas were located on the shore. The current light initially used the lantern from the previous lighthouse, which had looked over Conneaut Harbor. That is were the real story lies. Conneaut has a rich and little known history surrounding the lighting of the harbor.

Early in Conneaut's commercial life, the harbor actively exported whisky, lumber, and grain. To support this trade, the first light was established on Conneaut Creek in 1835. This was a pier light. From 1835 to 1885, pier lights alone were used to mark the harbor entrance. The first light tower was not built until 1885, when a simple tower was built atop a concrete crib at the end of the short pier on the east side of the mouth of the harbor. In 1897, the piers were extended, and a breakwater was constructed to slow the accumulation of sand at the entrance to the harbor. A new lighthouse as built on the north end of the new breakwall. These lights served the harbor until 1921.

In 1917, a unique, square two story brick and cement keeper's house was built on a concrete crib at the end of the extended east breakwater. A light tower extended from the northeast corner, making a third story of the building. This light became operational in 1921 and served until it was dynamited from its base and replaced by the tower we see today at the end of the west breakwater.

So, a light we looked at and deemed to be without sufficient "character" to include in this book proves to be very interesting. This 1921 light originally had an 11,000-candlepower light that emitted a beam visible seventeen miles out on Lake Erie. The tower base housed a diaphone fog horn that could be heard for about fifteen miles. The lighthouse was operated from shore by a keeper and two assistants.

The light was automated in 1972, and the lantern room was removed and replaced with a 375 mm beacon. Its alternating white and red beacon can be seen for 16 miles. The smaller East Breakwater Pier Light exhibits a green beacon visible for 7 miles.

The 1917 Conneaut Light is pictured here in a United States Coast Guard photo.

DUNKIRK LIGHTHOUSE

Type: Square pyramidal tower   **Established:** 1826   **Status:** Active museum

Location: Atop Point Gratiot in Dunkirk, New York.

GPS: 41 29.631   79 21.233

Access: Follow State Route 5 to Point Drive North in Dunkirk, New York. Then, follow the signs to the lighthouse.

Fast Facts: Shortly after the opening of the Erie Canal, Dunkirk proved to be the primary port city for New York's western coast. The first Point Gratiot Lighthouse was built in 1826 at Dunkirk.

Dunkirk Light

Photo by the authors

Story of the Light:

As with many of the light stations on the New York state coast, the Dunkirk Light was necessitated by the advent of the Erie Canal. Increasing water transport led to the Port of Dunkirk becoming the primary harbor for western New York, and the first light was established on Point Gratiot in 1827. This light and a pierhead beacon provided the range lights to guide vessels safely into the protected harbor at Dunkirk. In 1857, the original light was fitted with a third order Fresnel lens.

Time and the elements take their toll on a lighthouse. Standing unprotected against the winds of Lake Erie, any structure will eventually give way. In fact, there have been several pier lights marking Dunkirk Harbor. Two of these were destroyed by winter ice. By 1850 the Point Gratiot Light had developed a crack large enough to admit copious amounts of rainwater. This was patched and the light served for several more years. However, by 1874, wind and erosion from the pounding of the lake's waves had eroded the underpinning of the 1827 light, and construction was begun on a new facility. The foundation

Buoy tender and Dunkirk Lighthouse viewed from the water.

of the new keeper's house was formed from bricks from the original keeper's house. The existing cylindrical tower was moved next to the new residence, and a square tower was built around it so it would be compatible in appearance with the keeper's house. The new square tower stood 61 feet, 3 inches from its base to the cast iron ventilator ball on top of the lantern. Its focal plane was 82 feet above the mean level of the lake. It was fitted with the same third order Fresnel lens that had been used in the 1827 light. Adjacent to the tower was a fine, two-story Victorian keeper's house. These structures are the ones we see today.

The site is an active museum today and makes for a very enjoyable day. Visitors can not only climb the spiral stairs to the lantern room of the lighthouse, but also explore outbuildings and museum displays in the light keeper's house and the oil house. Also on the grounds are a 1926 steel lifesaving boat, a forty-five foot lighthouse buoy tender, the 1939, fifty foot tower from Dunkirk harbor, and a twenty-one foot tall 1929 tower from Grand Island, NY. One of the more notable attractions is the bottle light from Buffalo Harbor.

The light is still an active aid to navigation and the U.S. Coast Guard leases the grounds to the Dunkirk Lighthouse and Veterans Park Museum.

Grounds of the Dunkirk Lighthouse.

ERIE LAND LIGHTHOUSE

Type: Conical sandstone with brick lining   **Established:** 1867   **Status:** City park

Location: Lighthouse Street off of East Lake Road, Alt. Rt. 5. in Erie, Pennsylvania

GPS: 42 08.673   80 03.684

Access: The light is not open to the public but does have picnic and playground facilities in the surrounding park.

Fast Facts: The first Erie Land Lighthouse tower, built in 1818, shared the honor of being the first U.S. Government lighthouse on the Great Lakes with the Buffalo Main Light. It had to be demolished when it began to sink. In 1857, a second lighthouse was built. It only lasted ten years. In 1867, a new site was selected 200 feet east of the original location, and a new forty-nine foot tower was constructed.

Erie Land Lighthouse

Photo by Authors

Story of the Light:

There have been three lighthouses at the site of the Erie Land Light. The were built in 1818. This beacon and the Buffalo Main Light were the first U.S. Government lighthouses on the Great Lakes. The original tower was known as Presque Isle Light Station and stood a towering 20 feet high. However it was placed on a high bank overlooking the harbor. Structural instability was blamed when the first tower was found to be sinking. It had to be replaced in 1858 by a second light built 56 feet tall on the same site. When this tower also showed structural instability after only lasting ten years, the engineers were called in to determine the problem. Borings revealed a layer of quicksand hidden deep beneath the surface. To correct the problem, a third tower was built 200 feet to the east. This one was built of sandstone and had a massive foundation. Completed in 1867, the third lighthouse stood 49 feet tall and had a total of 69 steps to the lantern room. A two story "salt-box" style keeper's home was also built nearby. It was renovated in 1979.

The 1867 beacon is the one that stands today. The light's third order Fresnel lens guided vessels into Erie Harbor until 1881. At that time the light was deemed to be unnecessary and the property was sold. In 1885, after deciding the light was needed after all, the Lighthouse Board bought the property back. Not only was the light still needed but in 1897 the tower was raised seventeen feet in order to clear trees that had grown up around it. The light served for two more years before it was closed for good. The lantern room was removed, and the Fresnel lens was moved to Ohio's Marblehead Lighthouse in 1901. Finally, in 1934, the land was given to the city of Erie. The city created Dunn Park around the light and built a wooden replica of the lantern room in 1989. This restored the tower to its original appearance. As recently as 2003, a storm ripped the roof off the wooden lantern room. Fortunately, in 2004 the lighthouse was once again restored and a 155 millimeter buoy lens was installed in the tower.

The Erie Land Light is listed on the National Register of Historic Places (#78002397).

Coast Guard Station Erie circa 1900. From Station Erie scrapbooks.

ERIE PIERHEAD LIGHT

Type: Square integral block tower and dwelling **Established:** 1830 **Status:** Active

Location: Eastern tip of Presque Isle Peninsula at Erie, Pennsylvania. Enter Presque Isle State Park on Peninsula Drive and follow the loop road. Turn east on Coast Guard Road. Follow the road to the pier and lighthouse.

GPS: 42 09.368   80 04.264

Access: Although the light is not open to the public, the pier is a public walkway.

Fast Facts: The original 1830 wooden tower was destroyed in 1857. The 1858 replacement had a fourth order Fresnel lens that is now on display at the Erie Maritime Museum.

Erie Pierhead Light

Photo by Authors

Story of the Light:

Before the advent of settlers from Europe, the southern shores of Lake Erie were inhabited by Erie Indians. Their custom was one of living in harmony with the land as hunter gatherers. They stalked game and gathered plants from the forests, while fishing from the waters of Lake Erie. Legend has it that Erie Indians journeyed well out into the lake in search of the spot where the sun sank into the waters. Angry with the Erie, the spirits of the lake arose up in a ferocious storm. To protect his people from the spirits of the lake, the Great Spirit extended his left arm into the lake to block the storm's waves. What we now know as Presque Isle was created from the great sandbar that formed where the sheltering arm of the Great Spirit had stretched out. This bar provided a place of safety for the Erie, favored ones of the Great Spirit.

At the southeastern tip of this peninsula, the Erie Pierhead Light marks the entrance to this protected basin. The original Erie Pierhead Light was a wooden beacon built between 1827 and 1830. It stood for twenty-seven years before it was swept away by a sailing vessel that collided with it in 1857. The replacement light first shone in 1858. It is still operational today. It is a thirty-four foot tall, square, white tower with a wide black strip around the middle and capped by a black lantern room and walkway.

Erie Pierhead Light from the pier. Photo by authors

The original optic was a fourth order Fresnel lens, which was automated in 1940 and replaced by a solar powered light in 1995. The Fresnel lens was donated to the Erie Maritime Museum. The tower has been moved twice. The first move was in 1882, when the light was shifted 190 feet out on the pier. In 1940 the pier was extended and the light was moved an additional 509 feet to the east.

Back in the days when a keeper's services were required, the keeper's quarters were located at the Erie Life Saving Station.

Vintage photo of the Erie Lifesaving Station from the Erie Coast Guard scrap books.

ERIE PRESQUE ISLE LIGHTHOUSE

Type: Square integral block tower and dwelling   **Established:**   1873   **Status:** Active

Location: Northern tip of Presque Isle Peninsula at Erie, Pennsylvania. By car, drive Pennsylvania Route 5 and exit at Peninsula Drive. Follow the drive and enter the state park.

GPS: 42 09.949   80 06.913

Access: The light is not open to the public but it can be viewed from the beach and from public lands around the light.

Fast Facts: Constructed of brick, this light is now used as the residence for the manager of Presque Isle Park.

Erie Presque Isle Lighthouse

Photo by Authors

Story of the Light:

The first keeper at Presque Isle Lighthouse was Charles Waldo. On July 12, 1873, the day the light was inaugurated, Waldo's log read, "This is a new station and a light will be exhibited for the first time tonight - there was one visitor." He often described the Presque Island Light as the loneliest place on earth. We believe Waldo would have gotten an argument on that from the keepers at Mohawk Island and Long Point. However, until 1927, the only access to the light station was via a 1 ½ mile long sand path that led to Misery Bay. From there, the keeper could take his launch to the mainland in Erie, Pennsylvania. This "sidewalk trail" was paved by the state park in 1925 and can still be traveled by visitors to this day.

The Presque Isle Light Station was built to replace the Erie Land Light, which had been one of the first two lights placed on the Great Lakes by the U.S. Government. Construction started in September of 1872 and was completed on July 1, 1873. The forty foot brick tower was five courses thick and housed a fourth order Fresnel lens that could be seen for thirteen miles. The thickness of the tower was intended to hold back the ravishing waves in the choked channel between Presque Isle on the south side and Long Point on the north side of Lake Erie. The keeper's house was attached to and made an integral part of the light tower. In addition, there was an outbuilding to keep the whale oil that powered the light, which had a signature of two red flashes and four white.

After twenty-three years of operation, the tower was increased in height to fifty-seven feet in 1896. In 1927 a road was completed along Presque Isle to the lighthouse. Now, for the first time, the keeper could travel to the mainland without going down sidewalk trail and boarding his boat. About that same time, the light's signature was changed to an alternating red and white electric beacon. This caused it to be nicknamed the "flashlight" by Erie locals.

In 1962, the light was fully automated with a 250-watt white light. Today, it is maintained by the U.S. Coast Guard, and the keeper's residence serves as the dwelling of the Presque Isle Park Manager.

The plaque at the base of Perry's Monument honors Perry's victory in the Battle of Lake Erie.

One of the unique attractions of Presque Isle is the houses built on barges in Horse Shoe Pond.

This lighthouse alone warrants a visit to the area. However, Presque Isle is steeped in history and offers abundant wildlife. Misery Bay, at the end of sidewalk trail, is where Oliver Hazard Perry built the U.S. Fleet that reigned victorious in the 1813 Battle of Lake Erie. A monument at the end of the trail commemorates the victory. Directly across the bay, one can visit Perry's flagship, the reconstructed *Niagara*.

Presque Isle, French for "almost an island", is a sand spit peninsula sticking into Lake Erie from Erie, Pennsylvania. The park offers many trails, beaches, plentiful wildlife, and large sand dunes.

OLD FAIRPORT LIGHTHOUSE

Type: Brick keeper's house/ conical, gray sandstone tower   **Established:** 1825   **Status:** Museum

Location: 129 Second St., Fairport Harbor, Ohio - on a hilltop at the mouth of the Grand River

GPS: 41 45.522   81 16.668

Access: The light is an active marine museum open to the public. Visitors may even climb the tower stairs to the beacon room.

Fast Facts: The original light served as a refuge for runaway slaves. It was one of the first eight lighthouses on the Great Lakes and shone its beacon for 100 years. The Fairport Harbor Marine Museum is the first Great Lakes Lighthouse Marine Museum in the United States.

Old Fairport Lighthouse

Photo by Authors

Story of the Light:

Residents of Fairport Harbor often refer to the Old Fairport Harbor Lighthouse as "the light that shone for one hundred years." This light and its predecessor, which stood at the same location, did indeed shine for a hundred years (1825 to 1925). This light was more than a beacon of safe harbor for Great Lakes sailors. Standing 102 feet above the lake level, this tower also stood as a signal of safe harbor and free-dom for escaped slaves on the Underground Railroad. The citizens of Fairport were steadfastly antislavery and worked against the oppression of the Fugitive Slave Law. In 1850, Samuel Butler, owner of the Eagle Tavern, was chairman of a citizens' group that sought to repeal the law. The Eagle Tavern also served as a haven for escaping slaves and the headquarters for people willing to help. Ship captains, seamen, and townsfolk joined together to hide runaway slaves and smuggle them by ship to Canada. The keepers of the Old Fairport Light would hide escaped slaves in the lighthouse until vessel passage could be arraigned. All of this was done under the noses of Kentucky slave masters who roamed the streets of Fairport in a vain effort to recapture runaway slaves.

So, what is the story of the lighthouse that served the Underground Railroad? Originally named Grandon, this harbor had a reputation as one of the finest ports on Lake Erie. Because the river was a fair port, the town's name was changed to Fairport. The town and its river served as a stopping place for westbound settlers and vessels of commerce. Lake Erie storms can generate mountainous waves in a very short period of time. A calm and glass like surface can become huge crashing waves in less than fifteen minutes. As a result, in 1825, when Fairport's population was only 300 people, bids were requested for a lighthouse and keeper's dwelling. Architect Jonathan Goldsmith, won the construction bid for $2900. He completed the tower and keeper's house in the fall of 1825. However, there was a dispute over the cellar beneath the keeper's house. Claiming it was not included in the plans he had been given, Goldsmith submitted an exorbitant bid for the addition of the cellar. As hiring another contractor would be prohibitively expensive, there was no alternative other than to accept Goldsmith's price. This brought the total bill for the project to $5032, almost twice Goldsmith's original bid. In the fall of 1825, the lighthouse and dwelling were completed, and the whale oil fueled beacon was lit for the first time. Fairport's lighthouse was one of only eight lighthouses on the Great Lakes. It attracted more and more vessels until this "sailor's town" rivaled the port of Cleveland. It is this light that provided safe harbor for runaway slaves.

Within 10 years of its construction, the lighthouse showed significant signs of deterioration. The foundation settled to such an extent that a complete replacement was required. Within 30 years, the only thing preventing the lighthouse from falling over was wire hoops encircling it. Construction began on a new tower and keeper's house in the spring of 1870. The new light was built on a one foot thick concrete slab supported by piles which were bored over 11 feet deep. Above this was laid a grill of timber one foot thick, topped with a limestone foundation extending to ground level. The walls at the base of the lighthouse were almost six feet thick. This lighthouse wasn't going to deteriorate like its predecessor did! The brick keeper's dwelling and conical, gray sandstone tower were complete by the summer of 1871. A

third order Fresnel lens with a fixed white light was installed on August 11, 1871. Like the Underground Railroad light it replaced, the new light stood 102 feet above the lake level. It was visible for eighteen miles.

Progress sometimes brings unfortunate change. As vessel traffic continued to increase and steam power replaced sails, new piers and breakwaters were installed. The Grand River channel was widened and deepened. To service the changing harbor, the US Congress appropriated funds for a new combination light and fog station in 1917. This new light would be constructed on the west breakwater pier head. Although World War I delayed construction for several years, the new light was operational June 9, 1925, and it replaced the historic light that had shone on the hill above the harbor for a hundred years. Congress had also provided money for the demolition of the old light. Fortunately for lighthouse lovers around the world, this was not to be. People from far and wide came together to save the old lighthouse. The Daughters of the American Revolution, the Kasvi Temperance Society, the Council of Willoughby, Ohio, and the Painesville

The third order Fresnel lens is on display in the museum.

Kiwanis club were among the many groups that inundated the Secretary of Commerce with appeals to save the light. And save it they did!

The Fairport Harbor Historical Society has turned the lighthouse and keeper's dwelling into a Marine Museum. Visitors can immerse themselves in the place where runaway slaves once hid and devoted men cared for the beacon. Oh yes, we almost forgot to mention. The lighthouse is believed to be haunted by a gray cat, a pet of the bedridden wife of a past keeper. The remains of the cat were discovered in a sealed staircase in 2001.

FAIRPORT WEST BREAKWATER LIGHTHOUSE

Type: Square integral steel and concrete   **Established:** 1925   **Status:** Active

Location: Fairport Harbor, Ohio west breakwater

GPS: 41 46.072   81 16.867

Access: The light is an active U.S. Coast Guard facility and is not open to the public. Visitors may view the light by boat or walk the west breakwater by accessing it through Headlands Beach State Park.

Fast Facts: The appropriations bill that established this lighthouse in 1925, also provided funds for the demolition of the old Fairport Light. The proposed demolition caused an uproar around the lakes that led to the cancellation of the demolition orders. The West Breakwater Light stands 42 feet high and has an automated 300mm optic.

Fairport West Breakwater Light

Photo by Authors

Story of the Light:

The west breakwater light at Fairport Harbor has diligently watched over the harbor and vessel traffic for 80 years. However, the birth of this steel-framed brick lighthouse was not an easy one. In 1910 the management of navigational aids was transferred to the newly created Bureau of Lighthouses. This bureau was headed by George Putnam, who was reputed to be quite a practical and thrifty leader. Within months Putnam began tightening up the purse strings and making more efficient use of funds. However, owing to the rapidly deteriorating condition of the Fairport Harbor Main Light, an appropriation of

$42,000 was requested to improve Fairport Harbor. Funds were initially approved by the U.S. Congress in 1917. However, the demands of the Great Patriotic War (now known as World War I) delayed construction significantly. The new light would not become operational until June 9, 1925. When construction finally began, a portion of the light was actually built in Buffalo, New York at the Buffalo Lighthouse Depot , and transported 147-miles across the lake to Fairport aboard the barge *Wotan*. The actual tower and lantern room were built on site. George Putnam had saved about $10,000 by using this method of construction.

The "old" Fairport Harbor Lighthouse looks down the hill on the newer East Breakwater Light. Photo by the authors.

When first lighted, the west breakwater light replaced the Old Fairport Harbor Light, which had guarded the harbor for an even 100 years. Before the keeper moved in, the keeper of the Old Fairport Lighthouse had to take a rowboat out to the lighthouse to service it. While few townspeople objected to the improved light and its placement at the entrance to the expanded harbor, many resisted the idea of demolishing the old light. As a result, controversy surrounded the opening of the new lighthouse. Fortunately for lighthouse lovers, the old light was preserved and serves today as the Fairport Historical Society Museum.

Resting on a concrete pierhead, the west breakwater lighthouse was originally equipped with a fourth order Fresnel lens, flashing white, three seconds on and then three seconds off. The attached quarters housed the light keepers. Besides maintaining the beacon, the first tenders also cared for portions of the breakwater structure that allowed them land access to the light.

The *Wotan* brings Fairport's new light to town.

Today, the Fairport Harbor Breakwater Light is automated. The Fresnel lens has been replaced with a 300 mm optic. Though the keepers no longer walk her halls, this active aid to navigation provides a picturesque entrance to the Grand River and the towns of Fairport Harbor on the east bank and Grand River on the west bank. Perhaps the best view of the lighthouse is from Headlands Beach State Park and the Headlands State Nature Preserve in Mentor. Take Route 2 to Route 44 north. Travel Route 44 till it deadends at the entrance to the parks.

Long Point Lighthouse

Type: Octagonal concrete tower   **Established:** 1830   **Status:** Active

Location: Eastern tip of Long Point Peninsula, inside the Long Point Biosphere Reserve.

GPS: 42 32.923   80 02.963

Access: For all practical purposes, this lighthouse not accessible to the public. It is in a United Nations Biosphere Reserve, which is one of the most significant wildlife sanctuaries in North America.

Fast Facts: The current 97 foot high tower was opened in 1916. It was preceded by an 1830 conical stone tower that stood 60 feet tall and an 1843 octagonal wooden tower that was 75 feet tall. A keeper's quarters was once located near the light, but after the light was solar powered and automated, the quarters fell to ruins.

Long Point Lighthouse

Photo by Authors

With the possible exception of Mohawk Island Light, Long Point Lighthouse must be the most foreboding assignment a keeper could have on Lake Erie. It rests at the tip of a 25 mile (40 kilometer) long sand spit reaching down from the north shore of the lake toward Erie, Pennsylvania. This remote location is accessible only by boat, or in more recent times, helicopter. The keepers who worked this light often served additional duty as game wardens for the Long Point Company, a private hunting club that owned most of the point.

The first call for a light on the tip of this dark and ominous point of land came as early as 1817, only five years after the first Great Lakes lights were constructed by the British at New York and Niagara. Unfortunately for many lost vessels, this call from Legislative Assemblyman Cornel Robert Nichol went unheeded. Action would not be taken until four United States schooners went down in a storm in November 1827. Following this incident the U.S. Government insisted that the British Parliament build a light at Long Point. Some believe that the Americans had implied that they would take over the point and build a light themselves if the British did not comply. The resultant light first shone its beacon of 12 glass-tubed whale oil lamps on November 3, 1830.

Shortly after its inauguration, people realized the land at the tip of the point was in a state of constant change. In 1832, lighthouse superintendent James Mitchell reported that the point was moving to the south and the tip was rapidly extending eastward. It was already 220 yards further from the tower than it had been when the light was first completed! By 1836, when the first keeper died, the waves were quickly destroying the Long Point Light. However, it would not be until the spring of 1843 that a replacement light was begun.

The 1843 light was to be a 70 foot tall octagonal tower. The foundation for this light can still be found in the waters to the south of the existing lighthouse. The original whale oil lamps were converted to burn coal oil in 1864. While it took more coal oil to keep the light going, the coal oil was far less expensive than whale oil. In 1891, a steam and air powered fog signal was built next to the light. This rapidly became obsolete and was replaced by a newer version in 1900. Unfortunately, it took about 100 pounds of coal every 10 minutes to keep the sirens going in a dense fog. As the keeper was often consumed with his various other duties, it fell to the keeper's wife to shovel the coal.

The current lighthouse was begun in 1915 and went into service on May 26, 1916. The lantern room on the 102 foot tower housed a 100,000 candlepower light that was visible for fifteen miles. This light and the 1843 light stood together until the 1843 light was intentionally burned down by the keeper because it was on the verge of falling into the lake. In 1941, a crew of thirteen men arrived to install a diesel engine on the fog signal. While the keeper's wife may not have been thrilled about feeding these men for a week, she was most assuredly happy about no longer having to shovel coal.

Today, the Long Point Light is automated and maintained by the Canadian Coast Guard.

The 1843 Long Point Lighthouse is shown in this vintage postcard from the authors' collection.

LORAIN LIGHTHOUSE

Type: Square/integral. steel and concrete   **Established:** 1917   **Status:** Active

Location: End of Lorain west breakwater

GPS: 41 28.651   82 11.426

Access: The light is not accessible by land. It is viewable from the water and from the Lakeside Marina Pier on the east side of the harbor.

Fast Facts: The first light to be a beacon for the Black River was a lantern on a post. The current light is the second lighthouse structure on the river. It was nearly demolished after it was replaced by an automated light on the new outer wall and decommissioned.

Lorain Lighthouse

Photo by Authors

Story of the Light:

In 1842, author Charles Dickens sailed Lake Erie from Sandusky to Cleveland aboard the *Constellation*. On that trip, Mr. Dickens made note of the lights of the town of Charleston and its lighthouse. Those who are familiar with the Ohio coastline may well wonder where Charleston is. Truth be told, it is the city of Lorain. In 1834 the village at the mouth of the Black River was incorporated as Charleston. It was not until forty years later, in 1874, that Charleston was re-incorporated as Lorain. However, the light that Mr. Dickens noted is not the light that guards the harbor entrance today. That light, built in 1836 and 1837, was a cylindrical black tower capped with a small lantern room. This first light was replaced in 1875 by a light at the end of the newly constructed 600-foot pier reaching out from the west side of the Black River entrance.

As the light keepers made their daily trek to the light to take oil for the lanterns, storms often howled across the lake. These were particularly treacherous from the west and, on two occasions, lighthouse keepers were washed from the pier and drowned. As a result, a metal walkway was constructed on top of the pier to keep the keepers above the smashing waves.

Unfortunately, a lighthouse does not always keep vessels out of harms way. The Black River Historical Society documents several mishaps involving the Lorain Light. Two different ships are known to have run into the pier in 1890. The schooner *B.F. Bruce* damaged the elevated walkway on July 1, 1890 and additional damage was done by *Iron Boat No. 102* on July 24, 1890. The steamer *C.B. Lockwood* struck the west pier on the night of April 21, 1893 damaging the pier and one leg of the

This is the 1836 light that Charles Dickens would have seen as he passed by what was then the city of Charleston. Photo from Black River Historical Society.

beacon. The steamer *Caledonia* ran into the tower on November 2, 1894. On the night of June 24, 1895 the schooner *Mabel Wilson*, left lines tied to the legs of the elevated walkway while leaving the harbor. The legs broke and damaged parts of the walk. On August 16, 1895 three lens lanterns were shattered and the rear beacon destroyed by the collision of a ship being towed out of the harbor. And, on August 7, 1897 the schooner *Young America* rammed the rear range beacon. Talk about a bad luck light!

Given all the damage to the old light and range beacon, plans to build a new lighthouse that would include a place for the light keeper were developed in 1913. Construction started in 1916 and the lighthouse we know today was finally completed in 1917.

The Coast Guard assumed control of the Lorain Lighthouse in 1939. Three men manned the light during the two plus decades that the Coast Guard occupied the lighthouse. The light also served as a

lookout for the lifeboat station and for the Air Force.

Automated in 1960, the light was decommissioned in 1965. A simple tower with no character was placed at the western tip of a new outer break wall and the Lorain Lighthouse fell dark. As vandals decimated the once proud light, the Coast Guard first welded it shut and then made plans for it to be demolished by October of 1965. However this staunch guardian of the Black River would not go so easily. Lake Erie's notorious fall weather came to her aid as storms racked the lighthouse and the breakwater, causing the demolition to be delayed. This gave local advocates time to muster support for a "save the lighthouse" movement. This campaign led the Coast Guard to not only cancel the demolition, but also to declare that the Lorain Lighthouse had historical significance.

In the fall of 1981, "Operation Lighthouse" worked to refurbish the structure and professionally paint it using a donation of 160 gallons of paint from the Glidden Paint Company. An inspection of the building and its underwater foundation was conducted in 1987. The needed repairs were beyond the reach of the Black River Historical Society. The lighthouse was purchased by its present owner, the Port of Lorain Foundation, for $1.00. Since that time, enormous amounts of money, volunteer effort, and devotion has fueled the continuing restoration.

Today, this sentinel of stone and concrete shines as a lighted symbol of a gritty town that, like its lighthouse, fell on hard times and is striving desperately to survive. No longer dark and quiet, the Lorain Lighthouse is illuminated for all to see in the dark of night, and this "Jewel of the Port," represents the rebirth that awaits the City of Lorain, Ohio.

The *Calumet* passes the Lorain Light.
Authors' photo.

MARBLEHEAD LIGHTHOUSE

Type: Stucco covered stone and brick   **Established:**   1821   **Status:** Active

Location: West side entrance to Sandusky Bay at the tip of Marblehead Peninsula

GPS: 41 32.182   82 42.708

Access: Land access is via Marblehead Lighthouse State Park, just east of downtown Marblehead and behind the St. Mary Byzantine Catholic Church on Ohio Route 163.

Fast Facts: Marblehead Light is the oldest continuously operational light on the Great Lakes. Today, the Coast Guard operates a beacon, a 300 mm lens, that projects a green flashing signal visible for eleven nautical miles. The tower and grounds are maintained as a state park by the State of Ohio.

Marblehead Lighthouse

Photo by Authors

Story of the Light:

Arguably one of the most picturesque lights on the Great Lakes, Marblehead Light is the oldest continuously operated lighthouse on the Inland Seas. Commissioned by the 15th U.S. Congress in 1819, construction of the 50 foot tower was begun in 1821 and completed in only 11 weeks. Twenty-five feet in diameter at the base with 5 foot thick walls, the tower narrows to a diameter of 12 feet and the walls thin down to 2 feet thick at the top. The light marked the entrance to Sandusky Bay and the eastern end of the South Passage between the Bass Islands and the Ohio shore. It was called the Sandusky Bay Light until the name was changed to Marblehead Light in 1870.

Marblehead's Fresnel lens is on display at the Keeper's House Museum, adjacent to the lighthouse

Over her many years of operation, the lamps have been tended by 15 lighthouse keepers, two of whom were female. On the death of the first keeper, Benajah Wolcott, his wife Rachel Wilcott became the first female lighthouse keeper in the history of the Great Lakes. Mrs. Johanne McGee, was the second female keeper at Marblehead Light, serving from 1896 to 1903.

The beacon was originally lit with 13 Argand whale oil lamps with 16" reflectors. These were replaced by a single kerosene lamp and a Fresnel lens in 1858. It was this 42,000 candle-power beacon atop a tower of limestone that Civil War Confederate soldiers imprisoned on nearby Johnson's Island, could see from their bunk house.

In 1876 a lifesaving station was constructed one-half mile west of the lighthouse, and in 1880 the light began to take on the appearance she has today. A keeper's house was built near the base of the light, and the limestone tower was covered with stucco and painted white. She completed her metamorphosis in 1897, when fifteen feet of brick was added to the top of the tower. Now standing 65 feet tall, the tower gained capacity for a watch room and a more advanced lighting system. The lantern room was replaced by one taken from the Erie, Pennsylvania main light and a "clockwork system" rotating mechanism was added. It was driven by weights, which hung in a large pipe in the center of the tower. Although the mechanism was labor intensive (the keeper had to crank the weights back up to the top of the tower every three hours), the beacon's kerosene lantern now sat on a rotating table and was surrounded by a five-foot diameter Fresnel lens. This gave a 330,000 candlepower flash of light every ten seconds. This kerosene lantern would not be converted to electricity until 1923. The last major change

in the light came in 1969 when the tower's exterior was renovated and the beacon's 14,000-pound Fresnel lens was replaced by a 300 mm plastic lens weighing only 15-pounds. The tower's green beacon now flashes every six seconds and is visible for eleven nautical miles.

The Fresnel lens was placed on display in the Marblehead Coast Guard Station but in 2004 it was returned and placed on display in the completely renovated keeper's residence. Although the lighthouse grounds are open to the public year around, the tower is only open on second Saturdays in June, July, August and September. When the tower is open, you can climb the 87 steps to the top.

Viewed from the water, Marblehead Light looks like something out of a storybook fantasy. Photo by authors.

MOHAWK ISLAND LIGHTHOUSE

Type: Conical stone with attached stone keeper's house **Established:** 1848 **Status:** Ruins

Location: On a 1.5 acre island between Rock and Mohawk Points in Ontario.

GPS: 42 50.021 79 31.369

Access: The light can be viewed from the end of Pyle Road in Lowbanks, Ontario. The island is a national wildlife area and public access is not allowed during the breeding season.

Fast Facts: Although a preservation group stepped in to save the light from being demolished, nothing has been done to preserve it. The building has been heavily vandalized. The lantern room and the roof of the keeper's residence are gone.

Mohawk Island Lighthouse

Private collection of John Davis

Story of the Light:

The spark of interest in the lore of lighthouses comes from many sources. Although many people can't tell you when they were first drawn to a fascination with lighthouses, we can. For us, it was the Mohawk Island Lighthouse. We were researching shipwrecks in eastern Lake Erie when we first saw this wonderful light. It stood a lonely vigil on a small island located in a largely inaccessible part of the lake, one and one half miles offshore. It was magnificent and filled us with both awe and questions. Why was it there? Why had it been abandoned? On close inspection, the light was in ruins, and we had to wonder, why had it been forsaken?

So, what is the story of this forlorn structure in a remote corner of the lake? It was built in 1848 to guide vessels to Port Maitland, which was the original Lake Erie entrance to the Welland Canal. The first Welland Canal between Lake Ontario and Lake Erie had been designed to take advantage of the natural waterways of the Niagara escarpment. It began at Port Dalhousie on Lake Ontario and ran along Twelve Mile Creek to Port Robinson where it connected to the Welland River. From the Welland River, vessels could join up to the Niagara River, or follow a feeder canal that entered Lake Erie at Port Maitland. Construction of the canal began on November 24, 1824 and was completed by November 29, 1829.

From 1848 to 1933 the Mohawk Island Light, then known as the Gull Island Light, guided merchantmen and yachtsmen to the Port Maitland entrance of the canal. However, the canal had undergone extensive modification in that time. Five locks had been added, the feeder canal had been expanded, and a more direct route from Port Robinson to Port Colborne had been constructed. The canal had now become

43.4 kilometers long and 2.4 meters deep and consisted of 40 wooden locks. Most importantly, the Welland Canal feeder to the Grand River was not rebuilt. The Lake Erie entrance to the canal was now at Port Colborne, some 12 miles east of Port Maitland.

Regardless, the Mohawk Island Light remained in service until 1969. Located just offshore near Lowbanks, Ontario, all that remains today are the stone walls of its dwelling and the shell of the seven-story tower. Her first keeper had been John Burgess, a local farmer. Her last keeper, Richard Foster and his son, James lost their lives shortly after receiving a report that their home in Dunnville was on fire. The year was 1932. On receiving this news, the two men ignored a raging blizzard and headed for the mainland by boat. They were stranded on an ice floe and died of exposure. Their bodies were eventually recovered and buried on January 2, 1933. The following year, the light was automated. In 1969, as traffic in the area continued to decline, the light was replaced by a floating buoy.

Sometime in the 1970s a fire gutted the tower and destroyed the keeper's house roof. Today the island is a rookery for ring-bill and herring gulls, cormorants and rock doves. It is a national wildlife area, so tourism is not permitted during the nesting period April 1 until August 1 each year. The stone tower and small keeper's dwelling still stand on Mohawk Island. However, the ravages of time and the neglect and vandalism of man are taking their toll. The conical limestone tower has had the

lantern removed and only the walls of the keeper's dwelling remain standing. There is hope on the horizon for this once magnificent light. The Mohawk Lighthouse Preservation Association is working to restore the site. We wish them great success!

This poem was written to commemorate the deaths of keepers Richard and James Foster:

When we first saw this view of Mohawk Island Light from a distance, we were hooked on lighthouses.

Death Gains a Victory

Three days amid the ice and winds,
They fought their lives to save,
The sky o'erhead was dark with clouds,
And dark beneath their grave.
The slush ice closed about its prey,
Breaking with a thudding crash.
And when the anchor ice gave way,
It fell with dull, low splash.

Father nor son, ne'er thought to swerve,
As the boat drifted to and fro,
With weary heart and tranquil nerve,
Each felt his life's strength go;
Each felt his life's strength go and knew,
As time drew slowly on,
That less and less their chances grew--
Night fell and hope was gone.

Their bodies numbed by the bitter cold;
No, not a crust of bread;
No shelter from the angry blast,
A sand bank was their bed;
Oh, motherland, while thy native sons
Can live and die like these,
Keeping from shame that honored name,
As mistress of the seas.

~ Author Unknown

PELEE ISLAND LIGHTHOUSE

Type: Buttressed conical stone tower   **Established:** 1833   **Status:** Inactive, restored

Location: On the northeast corner of Pelee Island, Ontario at the entrance to the Pelee Passage.

GPS: 41 49.900 82 38.375

Access: The light is in Lighthouse Point Park, a 237 acre nature reserve. The island can be reached by a ferry that leaves Kingsville and Leamington, Ontario on alternate weeks.

Fast Facts: Once standing in ruins, this light has been completely restored to its original 1833 state by the Relight the Lighthouse Committee of Pelee Island.

Pelee Island Lighthouse

Authors' colection

Story of the Light:

Sometimes the hard work and dedication of a few good people pays off! The first time we ever saw the Pelee Island Lighthouse, we were visiting the wreck of the *America*, which lies nearby. Sitting at anchor on our boat, we were struck by the sight of the derelict lighthouse that marked the northernmost point of Pelee Island. The light was nothing but ruins. Her lantern room was gone and the wooden stairs that had once led to the top were broken and decayed. However, the fieldstone tower still stood as a proud reminder of the magnificent light that once guided ships through the narrow confines of the Pelee Passage. Today, thanks to the efforts of the Relight the Lighthouse Committee of Pelee Island, the Pelee Island Light looks just the way it did when it was first built in 1833.

This lighthouse, which once provided notice of the shallow waters to the south side of Pelee Passage, now anchors Lighthouse Point Provincial Nature Preserve. The preserve benefits from two distinct environments. There are wetlands in the Lake Henry Marsh and sand dunes caused by the flow of water through the passage. They promote a wide variety of plant and migratory bird species.

A fascinating story in the *Lighthouse Digest* Magazine tells us that Civil War general Robert E. Lee visited the lighthouse as a young man and killed the lighthouse keeper. It seems that Lee had been sent to the island to conduct a boundary survey and encountered the light's keeper, William McCormick. McCormick was not only the lighthouse's first keeper, but had also donated the land on which the lighthouse stood, and the stone used to build it. A quarrel broke out between Lee and McCormick and McCormick was killed. The article goes on to say, "Whether Lee was cleared of any charges or left before he could be charged with a crime is unclear to this writer, but local records indicate that Lee stole a few glass lampshades before leaving." (*Lighthouse Digest*, April 2001)

Another keeper, James Cummins, was honored with a gold watch for saving the lives of people from two different shipwrecks.

The Pelee Island Light was deactivated in 1909 and abandoned. Over the decades the light deteriorated to the condition in which we found it on our first visit. Fortunately, a ten year effort by the Relight the Lighthouse Committee resulted in a Canadian Federal Grant in 1999, which provided the funds to restore the beacon in 2000. This effort is a model for others to follow and an inspiration for all of us who are interested in the preservation of the rich history offered by the lighthouses of the Great Lakes.

Pelee Island Light before restoration.

POINT ABINO LIGHTHOUSE

Type: Four story square concrete tower   **Established:** 1917   **Status:** Inactive

Location: The lighthouse is at the end of Point Abino Road (a private road) in Fort Erie, Ontario.

GPS: 42 50.077 79 05.709

Access: The light is at the end of a private road in a gated community. It is best viewed by boat or scheduled tours that include a trolley ride to the lighthouse.

Fast Facts: Erected as a replacement for *Lightship No. 82*, which was sunk with all hands in the Great Storm of 1913, the lighthouse is nearly surrounded by water, and the land is surrounded by private property. Keepers had to wade through water to reach the lighthouse. This light was featured in the 1995 psychological movie thriller *Lady Killer*.

Point Abino Lighthouse

Photo by John Davis

Story of the Light:

This lighthouse was built to mark a dangerous rock shelf jutting out from Point Abino. In the late 1800s, fixed buoys were used to mark the shelf. Then, in 1912 and 1913 the rocky shoals of Point Abino Peninsula were marked by *U.S. Lightship No. 82*. However, *Lightship No. 82* and her 6 man crew were victims of the Great Storm of 1913, a "white hurricane" that swept across the Great Lakes. Lost when the lightship went down were Captain Hugh H. Williams, Mate Andrew Lehy, Chief Engineer Charles Butler, Assistant Engineer Cornelius Lahey, Cook Peter Mackey, and Deckhand William Jensen. The ship was raised and continued to serve as a Great Lakes lightship.

The Canadian government completed the current Greek Revival architecture lighthouse in 1918, and the keeper's residence was completed in 1921. The architecture of this light is unlike any other lighthouse on the Great Lakes.

Lightship No. 82 before the 1913 storm.

Her sculptured concrete offers wonderful details. The entire structure rests on a concrete island, with cement stairs descending to a narrow walkway to the shore. This was a tended light as late as 1989. The beacon was among the last Canadian lighthouses to be automated.

The Point Abino Lighthouse was deactivated in 1996. Since being decommissioned, the light has been designated as a 'Classified' Heritage Building by the Federal Heritage Buildings Review Office, as a National Historic Site, and as a Classified Federal Building. It is recognized for its unusual shape and classical detailing. However, a great deal of controversy began to surround access to the lighthouse. Canadians wanting to visit the lighthouse were not allowed on the property. That is because the land the lighthouse stands on is surrounded by the private Point Abino Property Owners Association, which, owns the road to the lighthouse. The Association denied access to all tourists, declaring that, "The road is really our driveway. We don't want people walking by our properties because they might be casing our homes for something to steal."

As long ago as 1923, the local township sought ownership of the road, only to be stopped by a Canadian Supreme Court ruling. When the city of Fort Erie first attempted to buy the lighthouse for $1 and assume its maintenance, they encountered Canadian law that said the property must be sold for market value, then estimated at $400,000. Fortunately for lighthouse enthusiasts, these difficulties were overcome. On May 2, 2003, the Canadian Federal government announced transfer of the historic lighthouse at Point Abino, Ontario, to the town of Fort Erie.

The entry road is still private, but Fort Erie offers guided tours to the public throughout the summer months. The tour includes a trolley ride to the lighthouse and a guided tour of the lighthouse and grounds. The original Fresnel lens can be seen on the tour, as it still rotates inside a 10-sided lantern room. We recommended that you get your tickets in advance by calling the Parks & Leisure Services.

POINT BURWELL LIGHTHOUSE

Type: Octagonal wooden light tower   **Established:** 1840   **Status:** Inactive

Location: 18 Pitt Street, Port Burwell, Ontario, Canada

GPS: 42 38.725 80 48.197

Access: The light is open to the public from Victoria Day weekend to Labor Day from 10am to 5pm from Tuesday through Sunday. In July and August it is open 7 days a week. Visitors can climb the 55 steps to the top of the lighthouse for a panoramic view of the harbor.

Fast Facts: This is the oldest lighthouse on the north shore of Lake Erie, and one of the oldest wooden lighthouses in Canada. It was restored in 1986 by Mennonite craftsmen using the same hand tools and techniques used when it was originally built.

Point Burwell Lighthouse

Authors' photo

Story of the Light:

When you visit Port Burwell in the off season, you'll find a total population of about 1,000 people. As you look around the town, you find a large number of impressive old homes and churches for such a small community. The presence of the the lighthouse makes one wonder about the events that led this quiet little town to have such an array of homes and churches.

A little investigation discovers that Port Burwell, settled first in 1803, was once a thriving lumber and railroad town. The lumber industry moved logs from the surrounding forests to Lake Erie via Otter Creek.

This made Port Burwell an important harbor for the transportation of timber. To support this trade, the Port Burwell Lighthouse was built in 1840. At the time, it was the only marker on Lake Erie west of Long Point. As such, it provided welcome guidance to safe harbor on Lake Erie's frequently storm tossed seas.

A mural decorates the Marine Museum.
Photo by Georgann Wachter

The simple octagonal tower had a whale oil lamp and a third order Fresnel lens, which is still in place. In later days the lamp was fueled by kerosene and finally by electricity. The light we see today was rebuilt by Mennonite craftsmen in 1986. They used the same types of tools that were used to construct the light initially, and restored it to its original specifications. Wooden stairs ascended the inside of the tower to provide access to the lantern room. They are supported by douglas fir and pine timbers that extend the full 65 foot (17 meter) height of the framework. Lap strake siding covers the framework.

Lumber was not the only staple of the Port Burwell economy. As the population grew, Port Burwell became the center of a thriving shipbuilding industry, and a primary commercial fishing port. Then, the extension of the railroad to the small port brought coal handling facilities and a cross lake ferry service.

Today, the timber industry is gone and the coal yards no longer exist. However, the light that once guided commerce to this thriving harbor has not gone dark. Decommissioned in 1963, the lighthouse is now owned by Municipality of Bayham, and managed by the Port Burwell Historical Society. The historical society still keeps the lantern burning to commemorate its past significance to early shipping along the north shore.

Across the street from the light, visitors can tour the maritime museum. It has exhibits of both marine and domestic artifacts. It also has one of the best collections of lighthouse lenses on the Great Lakes. Up the road summer tourists swarm the town's soft sand beaches. Local restaurants serve fresh caught Lake Erie perch and pickerel (that's walleye for you folks from down south). All in all, it is a wonderful way to wile away a summer day.

To visit Port Burwell Light, go south on Route 19 from Route 42 in the Town of Port Burwell. The lighthouse is on the right hand side.

Tower outside the marine museum.

PORT COLBORNE LIGHTHOUSE

Type: Square towers with red lanterns   **Established:** 1834   **Status:** Active

Location: On the breakwaters at the southern entrance to the Welland Canal at Port Colborne, Ontario.

GPS: Outer Light: 42 51.757 79 15.290   Inner Light: 42 52.051 79 15.172

Access: Not open to the public. The lights are best seen by boat. However, the lights can be seen in the distance from Lakeview Park in Port Colborne.

Fast Facts: The first lighthouse at Port Colborne was constructed in 1834. It was replaced in 1903 by the light on the breakwall on the east side of the canal, now known as the Inner Light. In 1928, the Outer Light was built on the west breakwall. Today, both lights guide vessels through the canal.

Port Colborne Inner Lighthouse

Photo by John Davis

Story of the Light:

The Port Colborne Lights mark not only the entrance to the harbor at Port Colborne, but also the Lake Erie entrance to the Welland Canal. As its ability to move cargo vessels up and down the Niagara Escarpment contributes to the economic growth and development of both nations, the canal is jointly operated by the governments of the United States and Canada. Approximately 40,000,000 metric tons of cargo transits the Welland Canal each year on over 3,000 ocean and lake vessels. Each of the vessels and all of this cargo is guided in and out of the canal's Lake Erie terminus by the Port Colborne Lights.

The Inner Light was built in 1903 replacing two previous lights located on the north breakwall. The Outer Light was built in 1928 on the south breakwall, and an old range light farther inland was torn down. The Inner Light is the taller of the two, with a tower height of 43 feet and a focal plane of 50 feet. The three-story pyramidal tower has an attached white building. The Outer Light is shorter with a tower height of 25 feet and a focal plane of 36 feet. It is a square, white building with a small room and lantern on the top.

The last keeper of the Port Colborne Lights was Al Kendrick. His wife's journal, titled *Al & Isabelle Kendrick Lighthouse Keepers* gives us a look at the life of a lighthouse keeper. She tells us,

> "I remember the Imperial Oil Tankers as they rolled and pitched in huge troughs coming into the harbor and rounding the outer lighthouse. In the fall the spray would freeze covering the dwelling with a thick coating of ice and the breakwater was so slippery that we were forced to stay inside for our safety. … The small bathroom downstairs had the only window other than the rear upstairs bedroom window in which one could see the lake and approaching ships, fog or storms without going outside. Al made me a stool to stand on as the window was quite high. On nights when visibility was questionable, I would look out that window dozens of times.

The lightkeepers manual says that the men operating stations on a 24 hour basis were only allowed to go ashore to get supplies and go to church and then only if a qualified person was left in charge and only if they were absolutely sure they could return. They were reminded that

their responsibilities continued 24 hours a day, seven days a week and on the Great Lakes 9 months of the year. On some stations in the 40's and 50's, the lightkeeper was only paid for the duration of the navigation season and no extra for vacation, isolation, or inconvenience. For some lightkeepers

Port Colborne Outer Light
Photo by John Davis

whose families lived on the station such as Long Point on Lake Erie or Main Duck Island on Lake Ontario it was a mixed blessing. The families could be together and younger children could be home-schooled. But as they entered high school, it meant separation until the end of the navigation season. Such was the unique life style of living on a light station that I expect those families would not have traded their experience for life on the mainland. Incidently, Al and I often talked about applying for a position at another station which included islands and northern locations. However, we were comfortable living in Port Colborne where I grew up and our children never wanted to move …"

In many ways, Al and Isabelle had it pretty good. If they could get to shore by launch or along the breakwater that led to the lighthouse, the town of Port Colborne has a lot to offer. Port Colborne is a small (population 18,500), friendly community that grew up around the canal. Visitors can enjoy the parks along the canal, shopping in the historic canal-side district, golf, beaches and museums, all watched over by the lighthouses of Port Colborne.

Both Port Colborne Lights viewed from the Pilot Boat
Photo by John Davis

PORT DOVER LIGHTHOUSE

Type: Square pyramidal tower with green lantern room   **Established:**   1846   **Status:** Active

Location: On the west breakwater at the entrance to the Black Creek at Port Dover, Ontario.

GPS: 42 46.864 80 12.100

Access: The exteior of the light is accessible by walking out the west pierhead from the base of Harbor Street.

Fast Facts: Port Dover was home to the largest freshwater fishing fleet in the world during the heyday of Lake Erie's fishery.

Port Dover Lighthouse

Photo by the authors

Story of the Light:

Built in 1846, the Port Dover Light was severely damaged when lightning struck it in 1981. With a tower height of 28 feet and a focal plane of 37 feet, it is not very big. However, it once guided the largest freshwater fishing fleet in the world to its home port. Today, the green light and electronic fog horn of this square, pyramidal wooden tower covered with aluminum siding, guide both commercial and recreational mariners to the friendly town of Port Dover. The tower actually had a part time keeper as late as 1979. Today, it is like most north shore lights, the Port Dover Light is small. The tower stands twenty-eight feet tall, and the focal plane is thirty-seven feet.

The area first saw European settlers when two French missionaries, François Dollier de Casson and Rene de Brehant de Galinée, wintered at the site of modern day Port Dover. The earthen remains of their encampment can still be seen near the fork of the Lynn River and Black Creek. A historical plaque marks the spot where their team of nine built a hut and chapel in 1670.

Following the American Revolution, British loyalists known as United Empire Loyalists, fled to the north lands still controlled by the Empire. By 1794, United Empire Loyalists had established the community of Dover Mills. This community was razed by Americans during the Warr of 1812. When reconstruction was begun, the settlement was moved to the mouth of the Lynn River. In 1835, the settlement was registered as Port Dover.

Although there had been a harbor at the mouth of the river since the early 1800s, the fifteen years following the establishment of Port Dover saw significant harbor improvements. These were necessitated by shipyards, a wool mill, and a nascent fishing industry. Among the harbor improvements was the construction of the Port Dover Lighthouse.

Port Dover remained small through the twentieth century, but her fishing industry blossomed, and the towns beaches attracted tourists. Many of the town's citizens were employed in the largest freshwater fishing fleet in the world, and were welcomed home from the lake by the glow of the Port Dover Light. From 1906 to 1993, the town was also home to Thomas A. Ivey and Sons, one of Canada's largest wholesale florists and rose-growers.

Although the fishing industry has declined significantly and Thomas Ivey and Sons has moved on, Port Dover's Light still welcomes thousands of tourists to the town and its beaches each year.

The Harbor Museum is housed in an original fisherman's net shanty, and commemorates Port Dover's rich fishing history. There are exhibits on the days of commercial sail, Lake Erie shipwrecks, ship building, Long Point, and the War of 1812. Since 2002, the museum has housed a collection of artifacts from the 1852 wreck of the sidewheel steamer *Atlantic*.

To get to the light, follow Route 6 (Main Street) to Harbor Street. Take Harbor Street till it ends. The lighthouse is at the end of the breakwall.

Vintage image of the Port Dover lighthouse

PORT MAITLAND LIGHTHOUSE

Type: Aluminum sided pyramidal wood tower   **Established:** 1846   **Status:** Active

Location: On the end of the west pier at the entrance to the Grand River at Port Maitland, Ontario.

GPS: 42 51.178   79 34.788

Access: The light is accessible through the park on the west bank of the river at Port Maitland.

Fast Facts: Working in conjunction with the Mohawk Island Lighthouse, the Port Maitland Light once marked the entrance to the Welland Canal.

Port Maitland Lighthouse

Photo by the authors

Story of the Light:

Originally called Green Cove, in 1869 the town was renamed Maitland in honor of Sir Peregrine Maitland, who was the Lieutenant Governor of Nova Scotia. Port Maitland's first wharf was built by a local businessman who needed to protect his schooner. However, it was the Welland Canal that brought a need for a lighthouse.

Sitting at the mouth of the Grand River, Port Maitland was once an entrance to the Welland Canal. The original lighthouse was established in 1830. During the second half of the 19th century, a feeder canal linked the Grand River to the Welland. Visitors can still follow the path of the feeder canal and see the remnants of it by following Canal Bank Road. This road extends from Port Maitland to the city of Welland and the Welland Canal. This feeder not only provided water for the canal but also provided one of the passages from Lake Erie to Lake Ontario across the Niagara escarpment. The lock at Port Maitland was rebuilt in 1904 and served the local area into the 1920's.

With construction of the second Welland Canal beginning in 1842, the present light was established in 1846 to mark the passageway from the Grand River to Lake Erie. At one time the Port Maitland Light-house was the front light of a pair of range lights. As a result, it is still commonly referred to as the Outer Range Light. When first built, it was a skeleton tower with only the upper part enclosed. In 1898 the bottom portion was enclosed. With a tower height of forty-one feet added to the height of the pier, for a total a focal plane of fifty-one feet, this green topped lighthouse is still an active aid to navigation.

Directions: Getting to the light can be confusing, mostly because there are two route 3's in the area. From Dunville, take Provincial Highway Route 3 to Queen Street. Turn southwest and go across the Grand River. Queen Street becomes Dover Road. Follow Dover to Port Maitland Road and turn left. Turn left again on Kings Road and follow it to the river. Turn right and follow the Esplanade Road to the park. The lighthouse is at the end of the pier in the park. You can walk the pier to the lighthouse.

You can walk the pier to visit the Maitland Lighthouse. Photo by authors.

PORT STANLEY LIGHTHOUSE

Type: Pyramidal concrete tower   **Established:** 1908   **Status:** Active

Location: On the end of the west pier at the entrance to Port Stanley, Ontario.

GPS: 42 39.304   81 12,794

Access: The lighthouse is not open to the public, and is best viewed by boat.

Fast Facts: On December 7, 1909, a Port Stanley customs official reported seeing the *Marquette and Bessemer No.2*. She was unable to enter the harbor because the waves were breaking over the light and obscuring the harbor entrance. This is the last reliable sighting of the *M&B#2*.

Port Stanley Lighthouse

Photo by the authors

Story of the Light:

The Port Stanley Lighthouse is an active aid to navigation, flashing a green light once every five seconds. The light sits on a skeletal tower atop a one story, square, concrete base. This white structure is located at the end of the west breakwater.

While the light itself can only be seen by boat, the surrounding town is also worth a visit. The outer harbor tells the history of the picturesque fishing village. Dozens of fish tugs line the walls of the harbor, and you can still get fresh catch along the wharf. Port Stanley is the largest inland federal harbor in

Canada. It attracts an impressive array of large lake vessels. Passing under the King George VI lift bridge, you'll enter Kettle Creek, a river filled with recreational vessels. You'll also see the historic railroad line on the west bank.

The area was originally settled as Kettle Creek in 1812. However, a visit to nearby Port Talbot by the 14th Earl of Derby, Edward Smith-Stanley, prompted locals to rename the settlement Port Stanley. Lord Stanley went on to become Prime Minister of England and to sire a son, Frederick Stanley, who donated the first Stanley Cup.

View of the historic King George VII lift bridge and the Port Stanley Terminal Rail line. Photo by the authors.

The lift bridge is the oldest of its kind in Canada. The town offers shops, beaches, live theater, and an amazing variety of restaurants.

Today, the lighthouse stands thirty-one feet tall and has a focal plane of thirty-seven feet. While it no longer guides the big railcar ferries into port, it directs recreational and commercial fishing vessels to the largest harbor on the north shore. However, if Cleveland politicians have their way, this little light may once again welcome ferry service to Port Stanley. Seven companies recently submitted proposals for a Lake Erie ferry between Cleveland and Port Stanley, Ontario. The Cleveland-Cuyahoga County Port Authority has announced that a Dutch company, Royal Wagenborg, is the first choice to provide this service.

The goal was to have begun service in the spring of 2006. However, negotiations for terminal construction, customs, immigration and ship capacity with both Cleveland and Port Stanley have slowed progress. The proposal envisions two vessels, one based in Cleveland and the other in Canada. At this point, it may be just a pipe dream. But, who knows, maybe one day soon we'll be able to take pictures of the Port Stanley Lighthouse from the decks of a commercial ferry.

Commercial fish tugs often crowd the harbor at Port Stanley. Photo by the authors.

RONDEAU WEST BREAKWATER LIGHTHOUSE

Type: Pyramidal concrete tower   **Established:** 1912   **Status:** Active

Location: On the end of the west pier at the entrance to Erieau Harbor, Ontario.

GPS: 42 15.194   81 54.527

Access: The lighthouse can be reached by walking out the west pierhead from the base of Mariner's Road.

Fast Facts: The Rondeau Light marks the entranc to Erieau Marina, which has docking facilities with water and power hook-ups for 300 boats and hosts about 3500 transient boaters every year.

Rondeau West Breakwater Lighthouse

Photo by the authors

Story of the Light:

The first lighthouse at Erieau was established in 1844. That same year piers were built, and Rondeau was officially declared a port of entry, complete with its own customs officer. At the time, Erieau was not much more than a sandbar along the shores of Lake Erie. It was a summer daytrip for people living in nearby Chatham, Ontario.

By 1887 the first cottage had been built, but visitors still had no land route to the area. Finally, in 1895, the first steam locomotive traversed the marshy approaches to Erieau on a rail line built by the Erie and Huron Rail Company. This opened the area as a summer excursion area and soon attracted regular ferry passenger service between Cleveland, Ohio and Erieau. With that service came a steady flow of U.S. vacationers and their money.

In 1876, the current East Pier Light was established. This square skeletal tower served as the front Rondeau Harbor Range Light until 1947. The tower was moved in 1891 and rebuilt in 1905. Today, the thirty-six foot tall tower, with a focal plane only one foot higher, is still in service, flashing red every four seconds. While the east pier is not accessible by land, the East Pier Light is easily seen and photographed from the west breakwater. A lighthouse behind the tower stood until it was demolished in 1947.

In addition to the tourists, the rail line brought other changes to Erieau. About 1898, the Pere Marquette Company acquired the rail line in order to use Erieau as a major coal distribution port. This forced the resort aspects of the village to shift slightly north, thus abandoning the west pier area to fisherman and mountains of coal. Because of the coal business, new concrete piers and a breakwater were added to the harbor.

The current West Breakwater Light was built in 1912. Located at the end of the west breakwater, this pyramidal tower stands twenty-four feet tall, and the height of the focal plane is a twenty-five feet. Flashing green every five seconds, the light is still an active aid to navigation. The following year, a project to drain 1,600 acres of marshland and build a road to Erieau was begun. A hard surfaced road was finally completed in 1938. Partially because of the improved access, Dexter and Herbert Goodison announced the formation of Erieau Drydock and Shipbuilding. Goodison boats would soon become the most popular commercial fishing vessels on the Great Lakes, and Erieau would become a thriving commercial fishing harbor. The most famous and largest vessel ever built by Goodison was the *Pelee Islander*, a 137 foot passenger ferry. The Erieau fishing fleet is still based at the entrance to the old coal dock channel.

The harbor began its transition to the recreation marina we see today in 1974. A longtime resident, Hartley Vidler, leased the entire property from the bay to the lake and east to the pier, from the Chesapeake and Ohio Railway Company, including the old Goodison shipyards. Vidler converted the harbor channel into a Marina that initially accommodated 100 boats. This attracted ever growing numbers of recreational boaters from Ohio, Michigan, and Pennsylvania. As a result, Vidler purchased all of the land except Kenterieau Beach and continued to develop this land into a fully operational marina.

In 1980, the Barnier family leased the old shipyard buildings and adjacent property from Hartley Vidler, and began selling and servicing boats as Barney's Boats Inc. The Barnier family has since purchased the entire marina. Today there are docking facilities for 300 boats and some 3500 transient boaters visit each year.

Erieau has gone from a daytrip beach, to a commercial coal dock, to a boatyard, to a recreational boating destination. What is next? Recently, local entrepreneur Roy Pickering acquired the land between the Erieau Marina channel and the Provential Park beach. He plans to build year round condominiums and single family homes on the site. After all these years, Erieau Harbor may soon have a more robust year round residential community.

The supply ship *Grenville* calls on the old Erieau Lighthouse. Authors' collection.

SOUTH BASS ISLAND LIGHTHOUSE

Type: Square brick tower with Queen Anne keeper's dwelling **Established:** 1897 **Status:** Inactive

Location: On the southern tip of South Bass Island

GPS: 41 37.730   82 50.475

Access: The lighthouse and grounds are not open to the public except during a tour at the end of August that is held as part of the Ohio State University Stone Laboratory open house. Visitors to South Bass on the Miller Ferry get an excellent view of the light as the ferry approaches the dock at South Bass.

Fast Facts: The light's two-story brick dwelling is attached to the square, sixty foot light tower. Topped by a round iron lantern room, the light had a fourth order Fresnel lens, but no fog signal. The light only operated from early March to late December.

South Bass Island Lighthouse

Photo by the authors

Story of the Light:

Although South Bass Island is best known as the anchorage of Commodore Perry's fleet during the "Battle of Lake Erie" in the War of 1812, it was the rapid expansion of tourism many years later that led to establishing a lighthouse on the southern tip of the island. Though the South Bass beacon no longer lights the night, tourism still thrives today.

The Lake Erie islands lured many settlers following the War of 1812, and commerce quickly increased. The islands produced limestone, firewood, timber, and grapes that needed to be transported to the mainland, but it was wine that drove large scale traffic to the island. As the reputation of the island's wine grew, tourism increased significantly. The peak of South Bass Island's popularity was marked by the opening of the Hotel Victory in 1892. The hotel drew even larger crowds to "The Wine Islands". The combination of tourism and commercial traffic through the South Passage (between the islands and the U.S. Mainland) posed great risk of loss of life on the rocky reefs and shallow waters surrounding the island.

On Feb. 15, 1893, the U.S. Lighthouse Board approved construction of a lighthouse and provided $8,000 to fulfill the project. Four years later, the South Bass Island Lighthouse was operational. It first cast its light across the waters on July 10, 1897. It continued to shine every night from March to late December until it was replaced by an automated steel tower in 1961.

The first keeper was Harry H. Riley. Riley hired a lighthouse laborer named Samuel Anderson who, two days later, committed suicide by jumping from the cliffs beside the lighthouse. Riley was so distraught that he went insane and was committed to an asylum. Mrs. Riley and Otto Richey were placed in temporary charge of the light while Riley's condition was evaluated. On February 23, 1899, Harry Riley was terminated with a terse note that stated, "Keeper Riley hopelessly insane."

The fourth keeper, Charles B. Duggan, also had an unfortunately encounter with the cliffs surrounding South Bass Island Light. On April 29, 1925, he died when he fell 30 feet from a cliff on the west end of the island. Duggan is buried on the island, in Maple Leaf Cemetery.

The last keeper was Paul F. Prochnow. He served from 1947 to 1962. When he first arrived, hugh iron weighs pulled steel cables to power the light's rotation. During his tour of duty at the light, the mechanism was converted to an electric powered motor. When Prochnow retired, the light was also retired and replaced by the steel tower that still lights the passage today.

Prochnow was awarded a "Distinguished Service" award by the U.S. Coast Guard, "for noteworthy initiative and skill beyond normal job expectancy". Perhaps it was because he was able to work the light for fifteen years without falling off the cliff.

South Bass Island Lighthouse is now owned by Ohio State University and is used to house OSU research and academic staff working out of Stone Laboratory. Located on Gibraltar Island, which sits inside Put-in-Bay, Stone Laboratory is the United States' oldest freshwater biological field station.

South Bass Island Light in 1897. Great Lakes Historical Society photo.

SOUTHEAST SHOAL LIGHTHOUSE

Type: Square concrete and steel on a pyramidal base   **Established:**   1927   **Status:** Active

Location: At the entrance to Lake Erie's Pelee Passage on the southern tip of Southeast Shoal.

GPS: 41 48.731 82 27.822

Access: Not open to the public. The light is six miles from the tip of Pelee Point and nine miles from Pelee Island, and only accessible by boat.

Fast Facts: After the Canadian Government stopped marking the Southeast Shoal in 1901, the Lake Carriers Association placed the *Lightship Kewaunee* on station. They manned and maintained the vessel from 1901 to 1910, using funds from the U.S. Government. In 1910 the Canadian Government again assumed responsibility for the station. Canada acquired the *Kewaunee* and used it until the Southeast Shoal Light became operational in 1927.

Southeast Shoal Lighthouse

Photo by Authors

Story of the Light:

Prior to the establishment of the Southeast Shoal Light, the tip of the shoal was marked by the *Lightship Kewaunee*. The *Kewaunee* was owned and operated by the Lake Carriers Association, which received operating expense reimbursement from the United States Government. All of this came to pass because the shallow shoal at the entrance to Pelee Passage is in Canadian waters, but the preponderance of shipping going past the shoal was U.S. flagged.

The *Kewaunee* was built at Kewaunee, Wisconsin in 1900. She was first placed on station for the 1901 season. This steam powered, wood, schooner hull was 90 feet long with a 24 foot beam and seven foot draft. Her light was oil fired and her fog signal was an eight inch steam whistle. After the Canadian Government resumed responsibility for marking the shoal, the *Kewaunee* was used to mark the wrecks of the *Joliet* in 1911 and the *Vidal Shoal* in 1912. She was then acquired by the Canadian Government and once again placed in service at Southeast Shoal. The vessel was retired when the Southeast Shoal Light became operational in 1927.

The light sits on an artificial island built on the shoal. To form the island, a large crib fabricated in Kingsville, Ontario was floated to the site, submerged, and filled with rock. Today's concrete and steel structure marks the eastern end of the Pelee Passage for upbound vessels and the beginning of deeper, open water for downbound ships.

William Moore was the light keeper from the time it opened in 1927 until his death on duty in 1950. On July 7, 1950, Moore welcomed the lighthouse and buoy tender *Grenville*. The *Grenville* was delivering gasoline for the sizable storage tank located on the lower level of the building. In addition to the fuel delivery, a great deal was going on at the lighthouse that day. The *Grenville* was also delivering a refrigerator, marine signals inspector Dowsley Kingston, and J.A. Arthurs, superintendent of lights and aids to navigation for the Canadian Department of Transport.

John Rice, second mate on the tender, had been overseeing the fuel tank operation but was called away to supervise moving the refrigerator from the tender to the lighthouse. There is some confusion about who was left in charge of the fueling operation, but Jack Urquhart, on board the *Grenville*, described what happened next, "I saw a flash come out of the door and Dowsley Kingston flew out of the door and fell between the lighthouse and the ship in the water." (Lighthouse Digest) Shortly after the explosion, William Moore fought his way through the flames and escaped, badly burned, through a second story window. Kingston had been working on an electric motor near the fuel storage tank when the explosion occurred. Captain Morpheth of the *Grenville* initially tried to fight the fire. He ordered his vessel to pull away from the lighthouse and battle the fire with the boat's four hoses. Eventually he realized that fighting the fire was a futile effort, and that the two injured people he had on board urgently required medical treatment. Both Kingston and Moore received first aid at the Leamington, Ontario docks before being taken to Leamington Memorial Hospital. The next morning, 64-year-old keeper Bill Moore died from his injuries. He left his wife, four sons and three daughters. That same evening, Dowsley Kingston also died.

No official cause of the fire was ever determined. However, it is believed that a spark, from the electric motor Dowsley was working on, ignited fumes from the gasoline.

The living quarters have long since been removed and replaced by a helipad now used to service the light. Those who have lived and worked on the light describe the pounding of waves on the steel sides of the structure as being deafening. It is as though the lake gods are slamming giant steel doors.

Smoke rises from South East Shoal Light after the July 1950 explosion. Great Lakes Historical Society Photo.

TOLEDO HARBOR LIGHTHOUSE

Type: Conical tower atop Integrated keeper's house **Established:** 1904 **Status:** Active

Location: On a manmade island 8.4 miles at 58°T from the mouth of the Maumee River.

GPS: 41 45.712   83 19.748

Access: The light is viewable by boat. Neither the light nor the island are open to the public.

Fast Facts: In 1986, the Coast Guard attempted to deter vandalism by placing a mannequin dressed as a lighthouse keeper in a second-story window. Local boaters quickly started a rumor that this was a ghost. It soon became known as the "phantom of the light".

Toledo Harbor Lighthouse

Photo from Great Lakes Historical Society

Story of the Light:

We are often asked if there are ghost stories about the shipwrecks and lighthouses on Lake Erie. While we are not great believers in ghosts, the Toledo Lighthouse is the home of the "phantom of the light". The phantom is actually a manikin placed in a second story window by the US Coast Guard. It is dressed in a light keeper's uniform and has been reported to beckon unwary boaters toward the rocky shores of the man made island on which the Toledo Light stands. We understand that new Coast Guard officers stationed at Toledo often sign the mannequin's shirt as a rite of initiation. For many years there were two uniformed officer mannequins but only one remains today. She has a blond wig and is fondly known as Sarah.

Standing guard over Toledo Harbor since 1904, this light has one of the most unique designs on the great lakes. It is a Romanesque structure, with distinctively styled Moorish roof. The light was commissioned after a deep water channel was dredged to link Toledo's Maumee River with navigable waters in Lake Erie. The light replaced the Turtle Island Light that had marked the entrance to the Maumee River since 1831. When the Turtle Island Light was established, there were approximately 200 vessels operating on the Great Lakes. As the size of Great Lakes ships increased, the five foot deep entrance to the Maumee River would no longer accommodate them. In 1897, the Corps of Engineers dredged a shipping channel through Maumee Bay. The Toledo Harbor Light actually marks the entrance to that shipping channel.

The 72-foot tower has a 3-story yellow brick house and an attached fog signal building. At the time of its construction, Toledo Light was considered the most modern lighthouse and fog signal station anywhere in the world. It had a 3 ½ order Fresnel lens with a 180-degree bulls eye, two smaller 60-degree bulls eyes and a ruby red half cylinder glass. A weighted clockwork mechanism made the light, which could be seen from up to twenty-four miles away, rotate. When construction began in 1901, there was no island, breakwater, or outcropping of rock to use as a foundation. The Army Corps of Engineers built the light in the middle of the lake by sinking a large crib below the water and filling it with stone. The crib was then topped with a concrete base, creating a man made artificial island.

The keeper's house and tower are one unit. It addition to the three story dwelling, there is a basement, an attic and watch room. The floors contain kitchens, sitting rooms, bedrooms and bathrooms for two lighthouse keepers and their families. They also house an office and the engine and power room. In all, there are 4000 square feet of space that is now empty.

In 1965/6 the light was automated but retained its 3½ order Fresnel lens. This lighthouse is still an active aid to navigation. Many commercial ships transit the channel throughout the busy Great Lakes navigation season. In the late 1990's the beacon's original Fresnel lens was removed and replaced by a solar cell powered 300 mm lens. While there is some debate about the location of the Fresnel lens, the Toledo Lighthouse Society says it may now be at the C.O.S.I. children's science center in downtown Toledo.

The federal government owns the site and does not open it to the public. However, the Toledo Lighthouse Society has plans to acquire the site. They intend to renovate it, and use the first floor and annex for public areas and displays, the second floor for research and education, and the third floor for emergency and other safety/training facilities.

The cylindrical tower is 13-feet in diameter, and the lantern room, with helical bar windows, is 8'6" in diameter. Look closely and you might be able to see the "phantom of the light" in the lantern room.

VERMILION LIGHTHOUSE

Type: Octagonal steel   **Established:** 1847   **Status:** Replica; private aid to navigation

Location: Vermilion, Ohio at 480 Main Street.

GPS: 41 25.503   82 22.024

Access: The light is viewable from the grounds of the Inland Seas Maritime Museum.

Fast Facts: The Vermilion Lighthouse was established 1847. In 1859, it was rebuilt and its 6th order lens was replaced with a 5th order lens. In 1877, it was once again rebuilt, and in 1893, the lighthouse moved closer to the end of the west pier in Vermilion. Ten years later the light was dismantled and replaced by an 18-foot skeletal tower. Finally, in 1991, an exact replica of the Vermilion Lighthouse was placed on the grounds of the Great Lakes Historical Society's Inland Seas Museum.

Vermilion Lighthouse

Photo by Authors

Story of the Light:

The Vermilion Lighthouse marks the entrance to one of Lake Erie's most picturesque harbor towns. Once known as the "Village of Lake Captains," the city was a popular drop off point for illegal liquor from Canada during the days of Prohibition. Vermilion is endowed with many beautifully maintained captains' homes in its historic Harbour Town District. Today, the Vermilion River teems with recreational boaters who are attracted not only by the historic town, but also by unique lagoons homes along canals constructed in the 1930s.

The same community wide revitalization efforts that have encouraged retention of the unique charm of Vermilion's businesses and homes led to the return of the Vermilion Lighthouse in 1991.

The earliest aids to navigation were established by local residents as Vermilion grew from a home for the Erie Indians to a bustling village in 1834. The townspeople would light the harbor entrance using oil burning beacons atop wooden stakes. By 1847 this tiny fishing village was catching the eye of business interests, including shipbuilders and commercial fishing vessels, so the U.S. Congress appropriated $3,000 to build a lighthouse and prepare the head of the pier on which it would be built. In 1852 Congress appropriated an additional $3,000 for repairs to the light and pier. In 1859, the light was completely rebuilt as a wooden tower topped with a whale oil lamp, red glass and a sixth order Fresnel lens. As was the custom of the day, a townsman would light the lamp each evening and refill its oil each morning.

By 1866, time and Lake Erie had taken their toll on the wooden tower and the decision was made to build a new light, this time out of iron, on the west pier. A home for the future keeper was purchased in 1871, six years before the new lighthouse would be inaugurated. The iron used to cast the lighthouse came from Colombian smoothbore cannons that were obsolete after the Battle of Fort Sumter. This led former sea captain and Vermilion historian Ernest Wakefield to opine, "The iron, therefore, of the 1877 Vermilion Lighthouse echoed and resonated with the terrible trauma of the War Between the States."

The new light was cast in Buffalo, New York and transferred to the lighthouse tender *Haze* for transit to Vermilion. The *Haze*, a steam-powered propeller vessel, departed Oswego on September 1, 1877 and headed west for Vermilion. Passing through Cleveland, the *Haze* took on the lantern, lumber and lime for building the foundation. She also loaded a crew to install the lighthouse and a fifth order Fresnel lens made by Barbier and Fenestre of Paris, France. One day later, the *Haze* arrived in Vermilion. Once completed, the tower measured 34 feet high. A 400-foot-long catwalk ran to the end of the pier, allowing the lighthouse keeper to travel between the light and the mainland even when large waves were breaking over the wall.

For over half a century, this sturdy tower shone its light for mariners. During this time, it was moved closer to the end of the pier (25 feet from the outer end) and survived many collisions with watercraft. Then began its decline. In the early 1920's, the Vermilion keeper's home was sold to the local Masonic Lodge. In the summer of 1929 two local teenagers noticed that the Vermilion Lighthouse was leaning toward the river and reported what they had seen to their father, Commodore Frederick William Wakefield. Within a week, the U. S. Corps of Engineers had dismantled this once proud lighthouse and replaced it with an 18-foot

steel pyramidal tower. The new structure was automated and no longer required a lighthouse keeper.

Sixty-two year later, Ted Wakefield, the teenager who had discovered the lighthouse leaning, would spearhead a drive to build a 16-foot replica of Vermilion's 1877 lighthouse. Wakefield's childhood home had been donated to the Great Lakes Historical Society and now served as an Inland Seas Museum. The replica light sits on the grounds of the Inland Seas Maritime Museum near the mouth of the Vermilion River. Erected on October 23, 1991 and dedicated on June 6 , 1992, the lighthouse is illuminated by a 200 watt incandescent light bulb with a 5th order Fresnel lens.

So, what ever became of the 1877 light? Surprisingly, the lighthouse was not destroyed after its removal. After being dismantled in 1929, the light was renovated in Buffalo, New York. In 1935, the lighthouse was recommissioned on Lake Ontario. It is still in service today as the East Charity Shoals Light, sitting off of Cape Vincent at the entrance to the Saint Lawrence Seaway.

East Charity Shoals Light, this light was formerly located in Vermilion, Ohio as the Vermilion Light.

WEST SISTER ISLAND LIGHTHOUSE

Type: Conical, rough stone   **Established:** 1848   **Status:** Active aid to navigation

Location: Southwest tip of West Sister Island.

GPS: 41 44.212   83 06.659

Access: The light is viewable by boat. Access to the island itself is restricted to research purposes only.

Fast Facts: West Sister Island Lighthouse is still an active aid to navigation. It is among the oldest lighthouses to survive on the Great Lakes. The light is not open to the public due to the threat visitors would pose to the refuge's water fowl nesting area.

West Sister Island Lighthouse

Photo by Authors

Story of the Light:

The West Sister Island Lighthouse was established on the westernmost point of West Sister Island in 1848. Her fourth order Fresnel lens marked the west end of Lake Erie's South Passage for nearly ninety years. This narrow passage between the Bass Islands and the mainland was the primary route for vessels transiting to and from Toledo and points east. The shallow waters and numerous shoals, combined with the narrowness of the passage, made for very treacherous waters. The beacon at West Sister provided mariners with a guiding light for safe voyages.

Although the tower was renovated in 1868 and a keeper's house was added, the conical limestone and brick tower standing 55 feet tall on a stone foundation is much the same as when it was built in 1848. The prime difference a visitor sees today is the absence of her lens room and lens. In 1937, the beacon was automated, and the keeper's dwelling was abandoned. A 300mm lens and solar power cell took the place of the Fresnel lens. In the same year, President Franklin D. Roosevelt established the island "as a refuge and breeding ground for migratory birds and other wildlife." The West Sister Island National Wildlife Refuge protects the largest wading bird nesting colony on the Great Lakes.

The death of her first keeper, John Edison, led to a dual tragedy. Martin Goulden, Edison's son-in-law, left for Toledo to purchase a coffin. He left his wife in charge of the light and traveled in the lighthouse's small boat. Halfway into his voyage, Goulden encountered a blizzard which, forced him to take shelter at the Toledo Lighthouse on Turtle Island. After spending the night at the Turtle Island Light, Goulden set out again the following day. He was accompanied by the Turtle Island Light Keeper. Less than a mile from the light, their boat was destroyed by ice, and the two were cast into the freezing waters of Lake Erie. Both men's bodies were later found frozen in the ice.

Despite having been declared a wildlife refuge, West Sister Island was used by the United States Army for artillery practice during World War II. While neither the wildlife population nor the lighthouse suffered significant damage, the keeper's

quarters were destroyed, and the tug *Custodian* was sunk. There are reports that fuel tanks, jettisoned by dive bombers, can still be found on the island.

If only the light could talk, it could tell us details of two West Sister Island rumors. First, during prohibition, rum runners crossing Lake Erie used West Sister Island for visual cover. Supposedly, when approached by authorities, bootleggers would simply drop their illegal stash overboard. While we cannot personally confirm the tales, the story is that bottles of prohibition-era alcohol are still being found on the bottom of the lake around the island. Second, and better yet, West Sister Island is often said to be the final resting place of former Teamster President Jimmy Hoffa. Speculation is that after he was abducted in Detroit, he was brought by boat and buried on the island.

In January 1975, the government designated 77 of West Sister Island's 82 acres as wilderness to be managed by the United States Fish and Wildlife Service. The US Coast Guard controls the lighthouse and five acres around it. The island is home to many varieties of birds, including great blue herons, great egrets, black-crowned night herons and double crested cormorants.

The West Sister Island Lighthouse is shown with the keeper's house in this
Great Lakes Historical Society photograph..

SHIPWRECKS

The *Mataafa*, aground and breaking up. Photo from authors' collection.

Shipwreck! Say the word and you instantly have someone's attention. What is this fascination with shipwrecks? Is it the challenge of finding them, the adventure of diving them, or is it the story each wreck has to tell? For us, it is all of these things and more.

When we first started exploring shipwrecks, it was a simple as enjoying being able to see underwater, and shipwrecks were something to see. From there, it gets more complicated. We have met many people who have a fascination with shipwrecks, but do not dive. We also

Stern cabin of the *George J. Whelan*
Photo by Jack Papes

know divers who, after a couple of visits to a shipwreck site, get bored with the wreck. Some of these divers move on to other shipwrecks, deeper locations, or stop diving altogether. Other divers can visit the same site dozens of times and still be captivated by it. They often take up underwater photography, videography, or archaeology. Can it be that these people and their non-diving compatriots see beyond the pile of debris lying on the bottom of the lake? Obviously the non-diving shipwreck enthusiast's fascination is driven by something other than seeing or touching the wreck.

We believe shipwrecks offer a way to touch a piece of history. It isn't the wreck; it is the story behind the wreck, the lives of the people who sailed on her. This side of shipwrecks mesmerizes us. To understand the events leading to the loss of the ship and the lives of the people who built her, sailed her, loved her, or loathed her is to know a shipwreck.

In our previous books, *Erie Wrecks East, 2nd Edition*, and *Erie Wrecks West*, we sought to bring some of this side of a shipwreck to the reader. This section of Erie Wreck and Lights visits shipwrecks that have been located since the other volumes were last updated. We hope you will find the stories of the wrecks as enthralling as we do. To preserve a wreck is far more than leaving it as you found it. It is preserving it in pictures and video, and documenting its story for others to enjoy.

E.S. ADAMS (aka: Samantha's Wreck)

Official #:	C33502	**Site #:**	**11**

Location: 33.7 miles at 1° T from Vermilion west breakwater light, 7.8 miles east of Pelee Point

Coordinates: GPS: 41 55.104   82 21.294   LORAN: 43862.5   57245.9

Lies:	bow northeast	**Depth:**	60 feet
Type:	3 masted bark	**Cargo:**	wheat
Power:	sail		
Owner(s)	Folger Brothers of Kingston, Ontario		
Built:	1857 at Port Robinson, Ontario		
Dimensions:	135' x 26' x 12'	**Tonnage:**	423
Date of Loss:	Tuesday, October 20, 1863		
Cause of Loss:	collision		

Talcott & Underhill capstan at Great Lakes Historical Society

Photo by Georgann Wachter

Story of the Loss:

Based on her location, size, approximated build date, and condition, we believe this wreck is the 135 foot long bark *E.S. Adams*. The *Adams* was built in Port Robinson, Ontario in 1857.

The weekend before her loss, the *Adams* had weathered a heavy gale from the southwest. The storm had set in on Saturday night and blown violently throughout the day on Sunday. Movement of vessels across the lakes came to a virtual standstill as a number of boats were temporarily stranded, and others were somewhat damaged, The schooner/barges *Arrow* and *Montezuma* went aground at Gross Point Light after fouling their tow lines and colliding. The yawl of the bark *Louisa* was destroyed in collision with another vessel, though no other damage was done to her. Other boats lost gib booms and had their sails blown out. All in all, considering the strength of the blow, very little damage was done.

Having outlasted the storm, the captain and crew had undoubtedly relaxed a bit as they hauled their load of Chicago wheat toward its final destination, Kingston, Ontario. Little did they know that the wheat was soon to become fish food. On Tuesday, October 20, 1863, the *Adams* was continuing her journey. In open water on a relatively calm lake, the *E.S. Adams* collided with the bark *Constitution* east of Point Pelee. One sailor, Nelson Hill, was lost in the incident. The *Adams* was reported sunk approximately five miles east of Point Pelee. The wreck site is 7.8 miles east of Point Pelee's location today. The point tends to shift as the beach comes and goes with strong winds and currents.

The Wreck Today:

This three masted vessel has one of the largest windlasses we have ever seen. Forward of the windlass, there are two, long-handled "J" hooked tools that were used to work the windlass. A large pile of anchor chain lies aft of the windlass on the starboard side. The large bowsprit is canted down into the mud and one anchor remains on the port side. The foremast has fallen to the port side of the boat, and a large portion of the port side and stern are gone.

There is a sizable centerboard. On the port side of this, a capstan with stars on the drum lays mostly buried in the silt. This capstan was made by Tallcott and Underhill of Oswego, New York. Their heyday was in the 1850s. As such, we suspect that this vessel was constructed in that time period.

Further aft, the sternpost rises out of the mud. Caution is required as fishnets abound at this site, and the visibility is often very restricted.

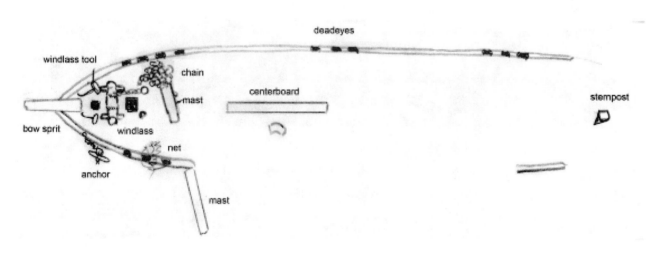

E.S. Adams
aka: Samantha's Wreck
135' x 26' x 12'
By Georgann Wachter
not to scale

The Admiralty Wreck / Schooner G

Official #:	none	**Site #:**	36
Location:	13.5 miles at 296°T from the mouth of Dunkirk Harbor		
Coordinates:	GPS: 42 34.612 79 35.002		
Lies:	bow west	**Depth:**	170 feet
Type:	two masted sailing vessel, most likely schooner rigged	**Cargo:**	unknown
Power:	sail		
Owner(s)	unknown		
Built:	appears to be of mid 1800s design		
Dimensions:	approximately 79.5' x 18.5' x 8'	**Tonnage:**	approximately 110
Date of Loss:	unknown		
Cause of Loss:	unknown but likely lost in a storm		

Cabin. "Schooner G". Lake Erie. 09/24/05. ©Jack Papes.

Schooner G Cabin

Photo by Jack Papes

Story of the Loss:

This wreck is commonly called *The Admiralty Wreck* because it was first explored in 2000 by divers who arrested the wreck under admiralty law in 2004. These divers believed the wreck dated to the mid/late 1700s and hoped they had found LaSalle's *Griffin,* the famous craft of about sixty tons, which was the first vessel to spread its sails on Lakes Erie, Huron and Michigan. A Buffalo commercial dive company was hired by Northeast Research LLC to salvage artifacts, possibly including: the compass, an old bottle, and what was described as the captain's six drawered bureau.

In 2006 the state of New York denied the admiralty claim, making the site available for recreational diving.

The Wreck Today:

As you descend to 60 feet of water, both masts can be seen standing. Although the top masts are broken off there are crosstrees on both. Even from this shallow depth, you can tell the vessel lists to starboard. Descending to the wreck and beginning at the bow, one sees a scrolled figurehead carving extending down and back to the hull. The bowsprit lies broken on the floor of the lake on the starboard side. On the port side, a metal stocked anchor lies on the deck. The samson post has a pyramid style top. The windlass lies immediately aft of this. A boom and gaff along the starboard rail suggest she was schooner rigged. However, the four deadeyes at the foremast may indicate she was built as a brigantine. Between the two masts is a small hatch and another hatch lies aft of the mainmast. Both masts have a fife rail around them. Surprisingly, though some of the cabin roof is missing, the low deckhouse is intact and the stairs and front hatch door are in place. A stove lies against the rail on the deck. There are two pumps at each corner of the cabin and two large square windows can be seen on the transom. Silt has filled much of the cabin and the hatches. As such, no cargo has been identified.

Since the vessel was tiller steered, we suspect it was constructed in the early to mid 1800s. With luck, by dating some of the artifacts and parts, *The Admiralty Wreck* will be identified.

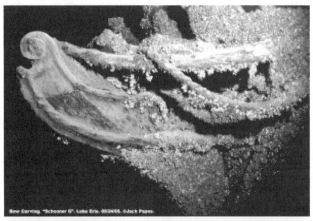

Scrolled figurehead, tiller, bow, stern windows, and yawl boat davit. Photos by Jack Papes

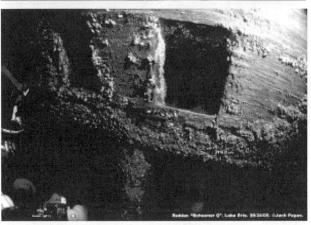

ALGERINE (AKA ALGERIAN)

Official #:	1085	**Site #:**	26

Location: approximately 300 feet off Raccoon Creek near Springfield, Pennsylvania, 3.5 miles at 68°T from the small boat cut at Conneaut Harbor.

Coordinates:	GPS: 41 59.553 80 28.958	Loran: 44216.7	58243.9
Lies:	bow west	**Depth:**	10 feet
Type:	two masted schooner rigged	**Cargo:**	iron ore
Power:	sail		
Owner(s)	F.S. Pelton & Boyce of Cleveland, Ohio		
Built:	1856 by A. Miller in Oswego, New York		
Dimensions:	133.3' x 25.9' x 11.2'	**Tonnage:**	300 gross 291 net
Date of Loss:	Wednesday, October 23, 1879		
Cause of Loss:	storm		

Story of the Loss:

The *Algerine* went aground and was involved in other mishaps on several occasions before her final loss. In April of 1860, near Oswego, New York, the schooner *Rising Star*, lost her bowsprit and headgear in a collision with the *Algerine*. In October that same year, she was carrying a cargo of barley when she sprung a leak in the Welland Canal. Her cargo had to be discharged at Port Colborne. In November of 1865, she was sunk at Port Colborne but later raised. In the spring of 1867 she hit the beach in Pigeon Bay, Lake Erie. The schooner also fetched up on and was lightered off Chickaluna Reef in Lake Huron in June of 1871. Later, in October that same year, she managed to arrive in Detroit with a cargo of coal, but her rigging had been severely damaged.

Her most spectacular encounter, however, was with a celestial object in October of 1867. According to the *Hamilton (Ontario) Times*, August 23, 1867:

DESCENT OF A METEOR

Capt. Turner of the schooner *Algerine*, who arrived in this city this morning, reports having witnessed at about the hour of 11 o'clock on Wednesday night, a terrible and splendid phenomenon in the descent of an immense meteor, into Lake Ontario, which struck the water not more than 300 yards from his vessel. The captain states that, a few moments previous to the appearance, he had come up from his cabin on deck, and was standing on the main hatch. The vessel was on the starboard tack, sailing along finely with a southwest breeze for Port Dalhousie, and about twelve miles off the Niagara Lighthouse, bearing SSW. Presently his attention was attracted by a sudden illumination from the northwest, which almost instantly increased to a dazzling brilliancy. On turning he beheld a large body of fire in the heavens which seemed to be approaching to a descent of about 30 degrees, and growing rapidly larger as it came nearer, the observation at a the time being so brief as hardly to admit computation in seconds. The momentary impression of Capt. Turner was that certain and complete destruction awaited his vessel and all on board, as the terrible missile seemed to be directed to strike the vessel broadside. The time for reflection, however, was brief, and the light emitted was so blinding in its effect that the man at the wheel and another of the crew on deck fell prostrate, and remained for some time completely stupefied with terror. The captain himself, as he states, remained transfixed and saw the fiery body enter the water some 300 yards ahead of his vessel, about two points to the windward. A loud explosion attended the contact with the water, which was sharp and deafening, equal to a thunderbolt close at hand, and a large volume of steam and spray ascended into the air, which was noticed for some moments afterward. In the confusion of the moment Captain Turner was unable to comprehend what had occurred, and the crew were inclined to believe that the phenomenon was an explosion of lightning, the sky being perfectly cloudless at the time. The captain estimates, as well as he was able to judge from the brief observation afforded, that the meteor was of about twenty feet in diameter. A long trail of flame of the most intense brilliancy was noticed as it struck the water. As Capt. Turner describes his sensation, his faculties for the moment were all compressed in the sight, so overwhelming was the light from the fiery object, but he believes he was sensible to a terrific whizzing, howling noise, similar to that made by the steam issuing from the escape pipe of a steamer, which attended the meteor previous to the grand explosion on striking the water. Capt. Turner arrived at Port Dalhousie on Wednesday morning. He assures us that his nervous system did not recover from shock experienced for many hours afterward.

Before the great Minnesota iron ore ranges were tapped, ore flowed to the west from Quebec and the Eastern United States. This was the cargo the *Algerine* carried to consignee C.E. Bingham in Cleveland, Ohio as she left Ogdensburg, New York. About half way into the voyage, the *Algerine* encountered a particularly vicious storm from the west. The gale force winds tore out the ships sails, forcing captain James Scott and crew to drop anchor and ride out the storm. As the storm continued unabated, the strong winds strained the anchor chains to the breaking point. The chains parted and the *Algerine* was thrown onto the beach.

Remaining aboard until it was certain that the vessel was going to pieces, the crew escaped in the ship's yawl boat. At some point during the ordeal, Collector of Customs H.S. Brown of Erie, Pennsylvania was contacted with a request that the revenue cutter *Perry* be dispatched to the aid of the stricken vessel. Unfortunately, the *Perry* was many miles away in Toledo, Ohio. The newspapers lamented that the uninsured schooner was, "In the days when fore and afters were the fashion, the *Algerine* was thought to be a fine craft." (*Detroit Post & Tribune,* October 25, 1878)

The Wreck Today:

This shallow water site off Raccoon Creek makes a wonderful skin dive. The *Algerine* is on a rock bottom with about 115 feet of her bottom intact. Chunks of her iron ore cargo lay strewn about the site. Deadeye straps and other rigging parts can be found and her anchor chain leads off to the north. Perhaps a search to the north along the track of the anchor chain might locate the anchor that was lost when the chains separated, allowing the winds to drive the *Algerine* to her final resting place off of what is now a small park.

An unknown two sticker, similar to the *Algerine*, ashore and being pounded by the waves.
Authors' Collection

BARCELONA SHIPWRECK

Official #: none   **Site #:** 34

Location: two and a half miles north of Barcelona, New York

Coordinates: LORAN: 44571.2   58791.5

Lies: bow west   **Depth:** 70 feet

Type: two masted schooner   **Cargo:** unknown

Power: sail

Owner(s) unknown

Built: appears to be of early 1800s construction

Dimensions: 62.5' x 17.5' x ?   **Tonnage:** unknown

Date of Loss: unknown

Cause of Loss: unknown

Barcelona Shipwreck

Cathead and bow post

Photos by Tom Wilson

Story of the Loss:

This little shipwreck was discovered in the late 1970s by side scan sonar expert Gary Kozak, during his search for the propeller *Dean Richmond*. At a later date, Gary provided the Loran location to charter captain Jim Herbert. Jim relocated the wreck in 1999.

Sensing that the site was very old, Herbert met with John Kuzdale, project organizer for Historic Harbor Renaissance, Inc. of Dunkirk New York. Art Cohn, director of the Lake Champlain Maritime Museum was also brought in as a consultant. The wreck was surveyed by local and LCMM divers in May and June, 2001.

The Wreck Today:

The *Barcelona Shipwreck* settled with her bow and starboard side down and more than half buried in the mud. The stern post rises approximately eight feet from the bottom of the lake. At the bow, the bowsprit is present, but it angles down into the mud. At one time there was a windlass on the vessel. All that remains now are the mounts for it between the second and third deck beams. There is a cathead on the exposed port side and two deadeyes opposite a partial foremast hole. A mainmast partner is thirty-five feet aft of the bow. The deck planking is gone, but the combing for the main hatch is present. The stern tapers to a robust sternpost with iron fish plates on either side. The rudder is either missing or sunk benieth the bottom.

Midsection of the *Barcelona Shipwreck*. Photo by Tom Wilson.

Since all of the standing rigging is missing or buried, it is hard to say whether this little vessel was a schooner, brig, or brigantine. Conclusions from the survey, published in February 2003 by the Lake Champlain Maritime Museum, suggest the vessel dates from the early to mid 1800s. Excavation of overburden might reveal artifacts that could be used to date or identify this small shipwreck.

The wreck is sufficiently covered by sediment and silt that it can be a very difficult target to see on a bottom sounder.

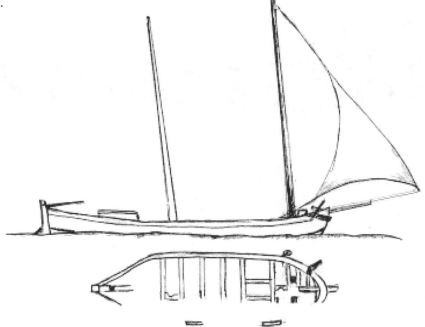

Drawing of the *Barcelona Shipwreck* by Georgann Wachter.

JOHN J. BARLUM

Official #: 76914   **Site #:** 9

Location: off Sandusky, Ohio

Coordinates: HOTM PA: 41 32 40   82 38 30

Lies: bow north   **Depth:** 45 feet

Type: wooden schooner barge   **Cargo:** coal

Power: towed

Owner(s) Pringle Barge Line

Built: 1890 by Craig Shipbuilding Company at Toledo, Ohio

Dimensions: 222.5' x 40.5' x 16.3'   **Tonnage:** 1,184 gross

Date of Loss: Monday, September 18, 1922

Cause of Loss: sprung a leak

John J. Barlum

Authors' collection

Story of the Loss:

John J. Barlum is the first of two vessels named after John Jerome Barlum. Barlum's father had begun a meat supply business servicing much of the Great Lakes Fleet. Built of oak, the *Barlum* had 13 large hatches to accommodate her primary cargo, iron ore. However, on the day of her loss, the *John J. Barlum* was loaded with coal as she left Sandusky, Ohio under tow of the tug *Guardian*. The trip to the upper lakes ended abruptly, when only five miles north of the jetty, the aging hull of the *Barlum* sprung a leak and settled in the shallow water. Her six man crew was saved by the *Guardian* and the *Golden Age*, another barge in the tow. After sheltering briefly at nearby Kelleys Island, the crew returned to Sandusky.

The vessel's masts stuck out of the 45 foot deep water, and her hull was only 15 feet below the water's surface. Lights were put on each mast to prevent other vessels from colliding with her remains. In October, a wrecking crew from Cleveland began working on removing her. By November there was a full 27 feet of water over the wreck. Finally, in the spring of 1923, she was dynamited.

The Wreck Today:

The exact location of this wreck has eluded several searches. She should be 3 5/8 to 3 3/4 miles off Sandusky Bay. As she was cleared to a depth of 27 feet by contract with the Hydrographic Office in mid November of 1922, and removed to low water datum in May of 1923, not much will remain. Also, we believe she is in the dredge dumping ground and on a mud bottom. Put all of this together and she's going to be difficult to find as she might be mostly buried so side scan would not readily reveal her location.

Resting on the bottom of the lake, the *Barlum's* masts still protruded above the water.

BRADSTREET'S DISASTER

Official #: none   **Site #:**   16

Location: one and one half miles west of Rocky River at Bradstreet's Landing Park

Coordinates: GPS: 41 28.99   81 51.85

Lies: widely scattered   **Depth:** 2 to 10 feet

Type: 25 bateaux   **Cargo:** military armaments and personnel

Power: rowed or sailed

Owner(s) British Military

Built: 1760 on the east bank of the Niagara River, at Fort Niagara (near present day Youngstown, NY)

Dimensions: 46 feet long (approximately 25 in number)

Date of Loss: Thursday, October 18, 1764

Cause of Loss: storm

Bateau

This small bateau replica sits outside of the Huron County Museum at Goderich, Ontario.

Photo by Mike Wachter

Story of the Loss:

At the end of the French and Indian War in 1763, the powerful chief Pontiac was organizing Indian resistance and attacking British forts in western Lake Erie. Late in the summer of 1764, an expedition under command of Colonel John Bradstreet left Fort Niagara to relieve the garrison at Fort Detroit. About half of Bradstreet's British regulars, provincial rangers, and friendly Indians were left in Detroit.

The expedition's return trip to Fort Niagara consisted of approximately 1,500 men in 59 long boats, several canoes, and one barge. Guided by an untrusted French pilot, the fleet left Sandusky Bay, Ohio on October 18, 1764. As the vessels approached what is now Lorain, Ohio, a storm was building from the southwest. Bypassing the safety of the Black River, the expedition rounded Avon Point and camped on an open beach. The wind then came around from the northwest, driving large waves that destroyed about half of the vessels and drowned some of the soldiers.

Ammunition and six brass 6-pounder cannons were buried to keep them from falling into hostile hands. Some of the boats were repaired at the nearby Rocky River, but about 180 provincial rangers and Indians, lead by Major Israel Putnam, had to march through hostile territory to reach Fort Niagara. Along the way, many bayonets, swords, and gun flints were discarded.

Just to the east of Rocky River, a mound three feet high by sixteen feet long produced skulls, buttons, and other artifacts. In 1842, a storm washed out musket barrels, part of a boat, flints, and brass trigger guards. Through the years, many items have been found on the beach or in shallow water near the shore. These include: a silver tea spoon, a French coin dated 1714, an English copper penny from 1749, a bayonet, and many stone canon balls. The Schooner *Victory* was supposed to retrieve the buried supplies in May of 1765. However, they did not successfully retrieve the munitions.

The Wreck Today:

During the high water years in the mid to late 1980s, we investigated the area with one of our dive clubs. The investigation found a bayonet, ring bolts, gun parts, and cannon balls. All of these artifacts were cataloged by the Ohio Historical Society. Many years ago, a small cannon was found in five feet of water. The divers had finished their dives for the day and were swimming and wading in the shallow water when they tripped over the cannon. The cannon is on display at the Buckeye Diving Center in Bedford, Ohio. Since there were six cannon buried "at the base of the cliff", it stands to reason that there are still five or six cannon somewhere in the area.

New artifacts occasionally turn up after a north or northeast storm.

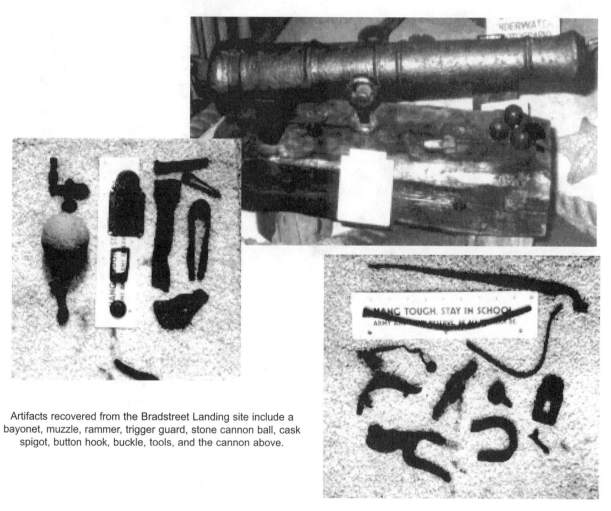

Artifacts recovered from the Bradstreet Landing site include a bayonet, muzzle, rammer, trigger guard, stone cannon ball, cask spigot, button hook, buckle, tools, and the cannon above.

BRIG C

Official #:

Site #: 37

Location: 6.4 miles at 370°T from the mouth of Dunkirk Harbor

Coordinates: GPS: 42 33.224   79 27.176

Lies: bow northeast

Depth: 115 feet

Type: two masted brigantine

Cargo: unknown

Power: sail

Owner(s) unknown

Built: mid 1800s

Dimensions: approximately 130' x 21'

Tonnage: 200 to 300 gross

Date of Loss: unknown

Cause of Loss: unknown

Brig C

photo by Jack Papes

Story of the Loss:

As this vessel is yet to be identified, we are unable to tell you the story of her loss. Rumor has it that this vessel was first visited by divers in the 1970s. At that time she rose 8 to 10 feet off the bottom. Since that time, a large amount of silt has accumulated. The silt covers much of the central section of the wreck, particularly her port rail, as she lists to port.

The vessel was commonly called *Schooner C*. However, the first time we had the opportunity to dive her, we counted eight deadeyes at the bow and three amidships. This configuration of deadeyes indicates she had square sails on her foremast, making her a brigantine (brig in Great Lakes parlance).

The Wreck Today:

The wreck usually has a tie in line attached to her starboard anchor, which rests against the starboard rail. While at the bow, you can follow the chain to her other anchor, which lies mostly buried along the port side. In the silt at the tip of the bow is the vessels cutwater. Scrolled carvings are present under layers of silt and zebra mussels. The bowsprit lays on the starboard side, perpendicular to the bow direction. A square samson post is arched at the top, and the arch is covered by a "U" shaped piece of tin or copper. The windlass spool has fallen out of its holder. A short distance behind this is the fallen base of the foremast with the end disappearing into the silt.

Amidships a large capstan peeks out of the bottom. Moving aft, the cabin is absent. There is a spindle

supported by a "U" shaped base. This probably held the steering mechanism. Behind this are three openings in the aft deck. One runs lengthwise and measures 2' x 4'. Along side this opening are two 1' x 1' openings. Fixed wooden yawl boat davits point back from the transom. Dropping over the heavily undercut stern, we find three windows just at the silt line. Some have the glass still intact.

Expect temperatures on the bottom to be in the high thirties to mid forties Fahrenheit. Visibility often exceeds 50 feet on this unique shipwreck. If you are lucky, you may catch a glimpse of a "dragon" as we observed a couple of 14 inch mudpuppies on the bottom.

View of the stern
Photo by Jack Papes

Starboard anchor
Photo by Jack Papes

Brig C
approx 130' x 21'
By Georgann Wachter
not to scale

J.J. CARROLL

Official #:	224735	**Site #:**	10
Location:	east side of Fish Point, Pelee Island		
Coordinates:	GPS: 41 43.547 82 40.261	Loran: 43734.9 57033.6	
Lies:	bow north	**Depth:**	10 feet
Type:	wood tug	**Cargo:**	none
Power:	gasoline engine		
Owner(s)	United Fisheries of Sandusky, Ohio		
Built:	1925 at Sandusky, Ohio by William "Mid" LaFountain		
Dimensions:	59.3' x 15.6' x 5.5'	**Tonnage:**	77 gross 68 net
Date of Loss:	Thursday, November 7, 1929		
Cause of Loss:	fire		

J.J. Carroll.

Historical Collections of the Great Lakes, Bowling Green State University

Story of the Loss:

One of the lesser known facts about Lake Erie is that, for a time, Lake Erie was home to one of the world's largest commercial fisheries. She has always had, and still has, the most productive fishery on the Great Lakes. In the heyday of commercial fishing, her catch typically exceed the combined totals of all the other Great Lakes. The peak years of commercial fishery in Lake Erie were in 1935 and 1956, when some 62 million pounds were harvested. To this day, despite large changes in species, fishing methods, pollution, and habitat differences, Lake Erie is one of the world's prime fisheries. Vessels like the *J.J. Carroll* built

Lake Erie's reputation as a commercial fishing powerhouse. In fact, when the *J.J. Carroll* was first built, she was said to be the most powerful fish tug on the lake.

In only her fourth year on the lake, captain Paul Brown and engineer Milton Witcher of Sandusky set off for the fishing grounds. Off of Pelee Island, the tug caught fire. While the cause is unknown, conjecture is that there was a short in the vessel's lighting plant. When the fire intensified, Captain Brown could not get forward to shut off her engine. As she drifted toward Fish Point, one fuel tank exploded. All of this happened so quickly that the two men did not have time to even use a fire extinguisher. They did however, make it safely to shore. Another fish tug, the *Grandon,* reported the loss and probable survival of the two men.

The same year as the *J.J. Carroll's* loss, the *J.J. Carroll II* was built. This slightly longer and even more powerful tug was washed ashore east of Fairport, Ohio in 1939. She had fouled her propeller while trying to assist another tug and scow.

The Wreck Today:

The wreck is about 100 feet from shore and just even with the tree line on the east side of Fish Point. Since she burned to the waterline, only a small section of her transom remains of the hull. However, more hull may be buried in the sand bottom. A barrel like object, closed at one end, is probably part of her boiler. To the east of this is a circular object about 3 feet in diameter and 2 feet high. Many pipes and metal parts litter this shallow site. Between the effects of winter ice and salvage efforts, this site is largely a debris field running north and south.

Expect 8 to 10 feet of visibility. In the late summer this shallow site may be heavily covered in weedy marine growth.

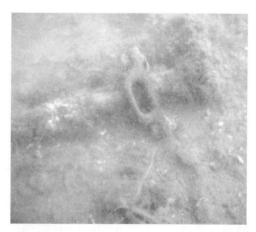

Piping, the boiler, and other metal parts are strewn across the bottom of the lake.   Photos by Mike Wachter

CATERPILLARS

Official #:	none	**Site #:**	28

Location: 35.4 miles at 7°T from Conneaut Harbor, Ohio.
20 miles at 120°T from Port Burwell, Ontario

Coordinates: GPS: 42 29.750 80 27.956   LORAN: 44436.5 58358.2

Lies:	east / west	**Depth:**	54 feet
Type:	construction equipment	**Cargo:**	not applicable
Power:	diesel		
Owner(s)	unknown		
Built:	unknown		
Dimensions:	the site is approximately 100' x 35'	**Tonnage:**	not applicable
Date of Loss	1990s		
Cause of Loss:	unknown		

Line Drawing of the Caterpillars Site

Georgann Wachter

Story of the Loss:

OK, so maybe we should have called this unique site Komatsu. We were so stunned at what lay on the bottom, and the seas were building to 4 to 6 feet, so you'll have to excuse us if we did not get the brand right. In any case, we started from Conneaut and took a small detour to a new wreck before checking this net hang. By the time we got the 30 plus miles out, the lake's waves had built to 4 to 6 feet. But once you've run that far and found something you cannot identify by the side scan images alone, it is time to go diving.

Dropping anchor (which of course did not land directly on the site), we each checked out the site one at a time while the other stood watch on the boat. Georgann went first as Mike was very concerned that the anchor would break free and strand us in the middle of the lake. After a brief dive, Georgann surfaced with descriptions of a unique dive site that forced Mike to leave the boat and take a look. Regrettably, neither of us took a camera on this first dive. You see, we descended down the anchor line to a sand bottom and 70 feet of visibility, and one of the most unique dive sites we have ever seen. As much as we wanted to stay longer and make additional dives, the building seas in such a remote area of the lake led us to believe that we had best curtail the diving and head for safe harbor. When we returned to this site the following season, we had calm waters and cameras but we were greeted with vastly reduced visibility making videography and photography very challenging.

So, what exactly did we find ...

The Wreck Today:

Sitting on a sand bottom in 55 feet of water, we discovered two construction excavators, one loader, a diesel generator, and parts of the house of a barge. One excavator was perfectly upright with its arm reaching 25 feet off the bottom of the lake. The loader lays on its side with the second excavator ramped up over it. Examining the top of the house, we found it was upside down on the lake floor and what appeared to be four motors were mounted on what would have been the ceiling of the house. A doorway reaches up from the housetop, extending about six feet from the lake bottom.

All of the equipment is heavily encrusted with zebra mussels, and there are metal parts strewn about the site. We were able to uncover what appeared to be a serial number on one of the doors and that number leads us to believe that the equipment is Caterpillar brand machinery. Since it was not marked on our chartbook in 1990, but was in the 2000 printing, we assume it was lost in that time period. However, extensive inquiry on both sides of the pond as to when this very expensive load was lost, and who lost it, has come up blank. We did received a vague "I think it was lost ten years ago" from one of our Canadian acquaintances. He said he'd get back to us after checking with the owner. When we followed up about a month later were advised, "I really can't say any more."

Hmmmmm. Now that's a real mystery!

Top of the barge house sits upside down with the doorway reaching up from the lake bottom.

Cab of one excavator with its arm disappearing in the distance.

Video captures by Mike Wachter

CHICAGO BOARD OF TRADE

Official #: 4331   **Site #:**   3

Location: on Niagara Reef, 10.2 miles at 348°T from the mouth of the Portage River, Ohio

Coordinates: GPS on the reef : 41 39.85   82 58.90

Lies: scattered   **Depth:**   variable

Type: schooner   **Cargo:**   coal

Power: sail

Owner(s)   L.S. Sullivan of Toledo, Ohio

Built: 1836 by Greenleaf S. Rand at Manitowoc, Wisconsin

Dimensions: 153' x 31' x 13'   **Tonnage:**   424 gross, 403 net

Date of Loss: Wednesday, November 21, 1900

Cause of Loss: storm

Chicago Board of Trade

Great Lakes Historical Society

Story of the Loss:

In order to facilitate agricultural commerce, a group of Chicago businessmen formed an organization named The Chicago Board of Trade in 1848. The bark *Chicago Board of Trade* took her name from this group, which is still in existence today. She was later converted from a bark to a schooner rig to expedite cargo handling.

It was a blustery fall day as the *Chicago Board of Trade* was making her way from Buffalo, New York to Toledo, Ohio. She had passed Sandusky Bay and successfully cleared the south passage between the Lake Erie Islands and Catawba Peninsula when a nasty November blow sent her crashing on to Niagara

This anchor was taken from the wreck of the schooner "Chicago Board of Trade," built in 1863, sunk in 1900 at Niagria Reef.

Reef. Her journey had been foiled by the shallow waters of Lake Erie's west end a mere 21 miles from the safety of Maumee Bay, her intended destination. The steamer *J.K. Secor* rescued Captain George Bonuah and crew.

Her owners dispatched the tug *Birkhead* with a lighter to remove the coal that had been bound for J.C. Schrenck in Toledo. The schooner *John Schuette* managed to remove only 100 tons of the 800 ton cargo when, on November 26, a 60 mile per hour northwest gale tore her bottom out and sent huge quantities of lumber ashore. This same storm wrecked the schooner *Saint Lawrence* as she sat at anchor just east of Lorain Harbor, Ohio.

A curious part of the *Chicago Board of Trade's* history was her sinking off of Fairport Harbor, Ohio on August 17, 1874. Captain McGraw, her owner at the time, had insured her for more than her original cost. Because of this, her loss during apparent fine weather proved suspicious, especially since the schooner *Hubbard*, another heavily insured vessel owned by the same captain almost came to grief a short time later. When the *Hubbard* was found to be leaking in Saginaw Bay, the vessel's steward observed the captain going below, followed, and found him making another auger hole in the vessel. Captain McGraw later stated that the *Hubbard's* captain was crazy. Insurance investigators did not uncover any misdeeds. These rumors continued to dog Captain McGraw fourteen years later when his lumber hooker *Fleetwing* was lost.

After her mishap in Fairport, the Coast Wrecking Company recovered the *Chicago Board of Trade* with

some difficulty in 1875. This permitted her to sail a few more years and to sink the *Golden Fleece* when she rammed her in 1883 on Lake Huron.

The Wreck Today:

CAUTION: This wreck lays at the corner of the restricted area for the Camp Perry Firing Range. Artillery shells in this area may be unstable and should not be recovered. Shallow water and hoards of fishermen are also a problem at this site.

The *Chicago Board of Trade's* keel lays in a dish formation at the bottom of the rocky Niagara Reef. Coal is scattered around and one of her anchors still sits at the southwest corner of the base of the reef. There is also some anchor chain on the southeast side of the reef.

Much of the *Chicago Board of Trade* is no longer at the wreck site. The vessel's cabin was used by locals as a chicken coop. Her rudder is in Toledo across from the Coast Guard station at the west end of a barn. One anchor is mounted in front of Wendy's Restaurant in Port Clinton and a second, along with other artifacts, is at the Sandusky Marine Museum.

An anchor removed from the *Chicago Board of Trade* decorates the entrance to the Sandusky Maritime Museum. Photo by Georgann Wachter

CLEVELAND CRIB NUMBER FIVE

Official #: none   **Site #:** 20

Location: 3.6 miles at 316°T from Cleveland Harbor entrance

Coordinates: GPS: 41 32.826   81 45.839

Lies: circular   **Depth:** 50 feet

Type: water intake crib   **Cargo:** water

Power: not applicable

Owner(s) City of Cleveland, Ohio

Built: 1914 to 1918

Dimensions: roughly circular 150' diameter   **Tonnage:**

Date of Loss: not applicable

Cause of Loss: not applicable

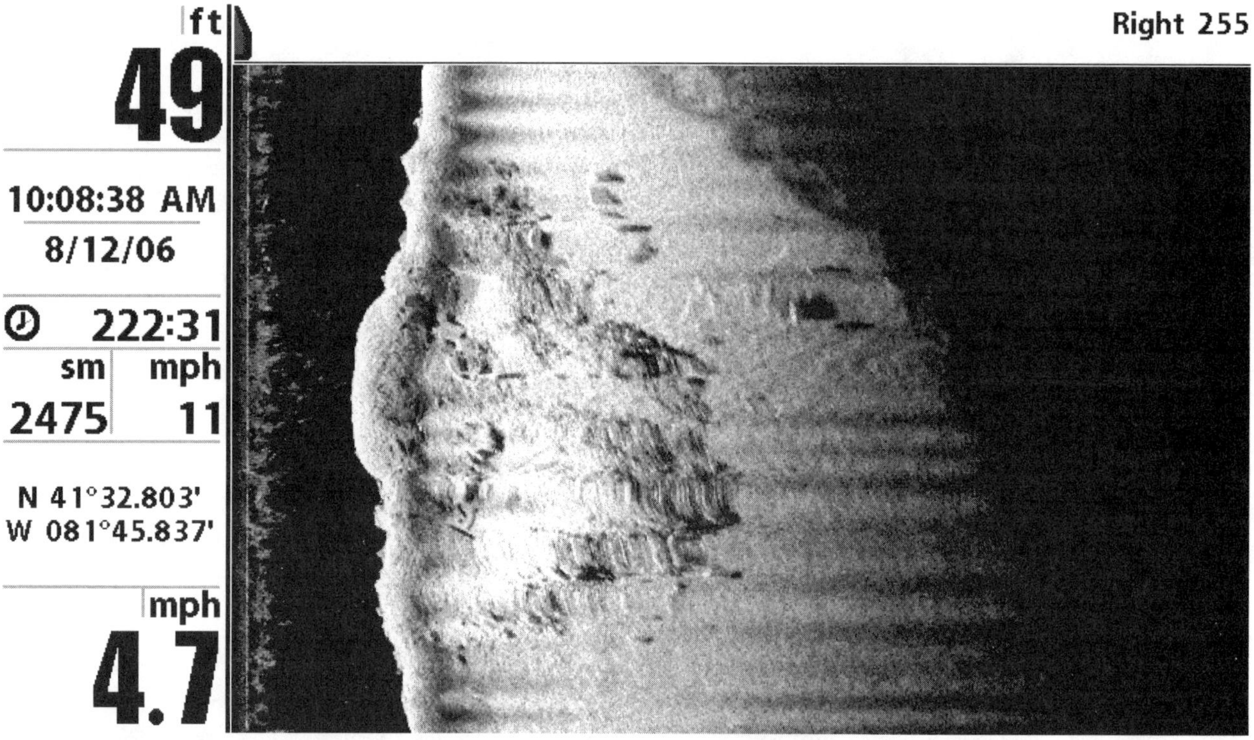

Side Scan of Crib #5

Crib #5 feeds water to the Garrett A. Morgan Water Treatment Plant

Side scan by Authors

Story of the Crib:

In the mid 1900s, the City of Cleveland was determined to supply fresh water to homes and businesses. The first effort was a simple, 300-foot pipe and brick aqueduct, that supplied downtown with drinking water. As the population grew, more elaborate water works projects were considered. Unfortunately, the liquid first carried in most of these tunnels was the blood of the people building them.

The first of Cleveland's five cribs was started in the summer of 1870, and completed March 2, 1874. It was a hefty timber structure, placed one mile offshore. The use of this first crib was terminated around 1900, and it was burned as a holiday spectacle off of nearby Edgewater Park. Building this tunnel cost seven lives.

Crib Number Two was built about two miles offshore and completed in May of 1890. Plans for Crib Number Three were formulated in 1896. A contract was awarded to Van Dorn Iron Works of Cleveland to fabricate a circular steel structure. In 1897, a large tank of steel, 100 feet in diameter and seventy-five feet high was built on the banks of the Cuyahoga River. On July 1st of 1898, it was towed three miles offshore and placed over the mouth of a five mile long tunnel. The bottom was filled with rock and a light keeper's house was built on top.

Construction of this crib and tunnel ended many workers' lives. There were two explosions. The first, on May 11, 1898, burned and killed eight men when a worker penetrated a natural gas pocket with his pick. Exactly two months later another, similar explosion killed eleven tunnel

shaft below the crib. One of these men suffocated. The rest were rescued hours later. Three men had been given up as lost, but five days after the incident, tapping was heard on the air pipes. Rescuers were lowered into a shaft, and John Eugine and Adam Kent were brought out bleeding, hypothermic and almost starved to death.

A day after this rescue, five men were buried, and one killed by a fall when crib number three exploded. The lake flooded the project. It was not until morning that the survivors were able to attract attention to their plight.

Four more were lost in December of 1904. Counting a number of laborers who died of "caisson" disease, or the "bends", the death toll was almost seventy before work was completed in 1904.

On August 3, 1914, the City of Cleveland decided

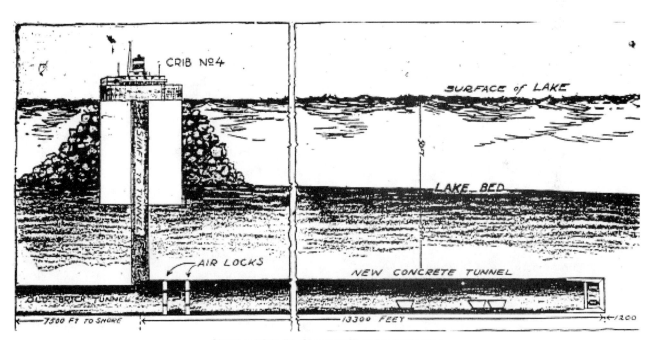

Cleveland Crib #4, *Cleveland Plain Dealer* drawing

diggers. After the bodies were recovered, temporary cribs were set up further out, and work resumed on the shaft.

One of these temporary cribs burned on August 14, 1901. There had been forty men sleeping on the crib at the time. Five men died in the flames, and five others drowned as they fled the fire by jumping into the lake.

Nine workers were trapped in the bottom of the

to extend the 1874 and 1890 tunnels some three miles offshore. Because of the excessive loss of life connected with the third crib, the city planned to do the work itself. For almost two years, officials and engineers were confident that this water works project would be completed without loss of life. Then, disaster struck. On Monday evening, July 24, 1916, an explosion tore through a ten foot diameter tunnel. It was 128 feet below the surface

The fire tug *George A. Wallace* brings victims to shore. *Plain Dealer*, July 24, 1966

notified the lifesavers of rockets over the lake. Survivors of the disaster were desperately trying to attract attention to their plight. The passing freighter, *Star of Jupiter*, was first to respond. They were followed quickly by the Cleveland llifesavers. Two injured men were transported to Lakeside Hospital.

Superintendent Van Duzen was notified at 12:30am that something terrible had happened at Crib Number Five. He rushed to the shore and boarded the tug *Lorain*. By then, several valiant coworkers had recklessly entered the shaft to try to free their eleven comrades. They died for their efforts. Once on the crib, Van Duzen and several more men entered the hole, and were soon overcome by the gas. Mrs. Van Duzen had asked her taxi driver son, Tom Clancy, to follow his stepfather's boat out to the worksite. At 3am, Tom had boarded the tug *Gillmore* with utilities director Thomas Farrell, water commissioner Jaeger, and two newsmen. Their arrival at the crib was greeted with frenzied cries from the surviving crib workers for helmets and Pulmotors. Tom Clancy and Jim Keeling insisted on boarding the lift and entering the shaft. As they went in the hole, one old timer agonized that, now two more were going to die.

A while later, the lift bounced up the shaft. In the small car were three men, with Clancy and Keating lying on top of them. The three workers could not be revived. The two heroic men

of Lake Erie, and inshore from Crib Number Five.

The previous Saturday, shield driver William C. Moore had discovered a one foot hole with gas roaring out of it. He notified officials. One gang of workers went down Sunday evening, but had to quit early because of the leak. A later gang refused to descend down into the shaft. On Monday evening, Superintendent Gustav Van Duzen checked, and found only a small amount of gas. The decision was made to send Harry Vokes' gang in early, at 8pm on Monday, so they could get the shift in. An explosion roared through the tunnel.

At 11:30pm on Monday, a resident on shore

Crib Number 5 as it appeared at the time of the disaster. *Plain Dealer*, July 24, 1966

Garrett A. Morgan

Inventor of the gas mask and hero of the *Crib 5* disaster

quickly recovered and screamed to go back down. They could see trapped men, including Clancy's stepfather, through the bull's eye in the air lock. They were allowed to descend again. Once at the tunnel, they smashed the glass bull's eye to admit air to the unconscious workers on the other side. On this trip, they rescued superintendent Van Duzen.

Meanwhile, at one in the morning, the phone rang in the home of Garrett Morgan, the African American inventor of the gas mask. Morgan woke his brother, Frank. Gathering a dozen masks, they hurried to the waterfront. Some seven hours after the explosion, the gas masks finally arrived at Crib Number Five. Once on the crib, Garrett and Frank were asked if they would go down to the tunnel, and they agreed. At the bottom of the shaft, the two men heard frantic pounding on the lock door. The Morgans were unable to open the door until they smashed the glass peep hole. One man was quickly brought up on the elevator. The two rescuers were joined by others, and brought up five more men before someone from the bureau of mines closed down the operation. Of the six men brought up, only two lived.

It was days before the bodies of the eleven buried men in the cave in were recovered. Ten other "sandhogs" had succumbed to the gas fumes, and nine were hospitalized, all in the effort to supply fresh drinking water to a growing city.

The Crib Today:

At one time, Crib Number Five was capped by a square tower that that emerged from the lake. Workers ate and slept in shanties constructed on top of this man made island. Today, this crib rests on the bottom of the lake in fifty feet of water. A circular pile of stone, roughly 150 feet in diameter, rises twenty-one feet off the bottom. In 1961, the

Crib #3 is better known as th "Five Mile Crib" because it is five miles from the water treatment plant.

Army Corp of Engineers, fearing that a deep draft vessel would hit these rocks, required the City of Cleveland to mark it with an obstruction buoy. This buoy, marked CWD is west of the crib. The intake is capped by a twenty foot square grate, set inside the rocks. We first investigated this site because it was alleged that a shipwreck was on top of the crib. We can find no archival evidence of this, but it is an interesting dive, with timbers, spikes, wood grates, metal rails, and large diameter chain snaking down the stone mountain. This debris is probably from the demolition of the coffer dam around the intake.

Number Three Crib, with a house, fog horn, and beacon is about one mile east of this submerged crib.

This site has heavy recreational and commercial boat traffic.

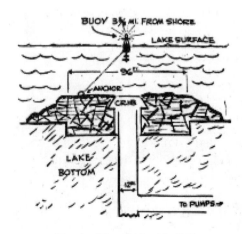

Cleveland Press, May 12, 1961

COMMODORE

Official #: 125805   **Site #:** 12

Location: on the Canada and United States border north of Lorain, Ohio

Coordinates: GPS PA: 41 42.8   82 18.9

Lies: **Depth:** 65 feet

Type: barge, two masts   **Cargo:** coal

Power: towed

Owner(s) Frank Desot with Clarance LeBeau, Manager, Citizens Sand and Gravel Company, Toledo, Ohio

Built: 1880 by Thomas Arnold at Carrolton, Michigan

Dimensions: 170.8' x 33.8' x 11.8'   **Tonnage:** 550 gross, 510 net

Date of Loss: Monday, June 17, 1918

Cause of Loss: storm

Commodore

Authors' Collection

Story of the Loss:

The oak hulled *Commodore* was built as a schooner in 1880 but was converted to a barge in North Tonawanda, New York in 1912. She had a narrow escape on Lake Superior in late September of 1895. The steamer *P.H. Birkhead* had the *Commodore* and two other schooner barges, the *Elma* and the *Charles B. Jones,* in tow when she was mauled by a storm and the lines parted. The *Commodore* made the Soo on her shortened sails, while the *Jones* anchored for two days in mountainous waves and the *Elma* crashed ashore, killing one sailor.

On another occasion, she was waterlogged and scuttled near Thunder Bay in Lake Huron. This occurred on October 11, 1915.

The steamer *Jay Gould* and consort barge *Commodore* ran a regular route between Cleveland and Sandwich, Ontario in the coal trade for the Pittsburgh Coal Company. The steamer departed Cleveland at noon on Monday, June 17th and headed into heavy seas with thirty mile per hour winds. The forty-nine year old steamer began to leak, so she dropped the tow line, setting the *Commodore* free. The bilge pumps on the *Gould* would not keep up with the rising water. Finally, after the water was over the knees of the engine room crew Captain James McCauley ordered the crew on deck. Her twenty-two men were rescued by the steamer *Midvale* and landed in Ashtabula.

Sandusky Register, June 20, 1918

Meanwhile, the *Commodore* was taking water and rolling uncontrollably in the trough of the sea. It was about 7:30pm when she was cut loose from the steamer. About two hours later, the *Commodore's* crew of four men and three women boarded a lifeboat. They were floating alongside the waterlogged barge when it settled to the bottom of Lake Erie. The steamer *Mataafa*, under command of Captain D. Elliot and towing the *T.L. Bell* had noticed their plight. They were able to get Captain Booth and the rest of the *Commodore's* crew on board. In the pitching waves, the barge *Bell* was damaged. The crew of the *Commodore* was landed in Sandwich, Ontario.

Much debris from both vessels came ashore at Kelleys Island.

The Wreck Today

The *Commodore* sits on a soft bottom with a slight list to the port side. Her two huge, woodstock anchors are still in place. The vessel's donkey boiler is at the bow and still has the builders plate attached. There is a very nice iron bell, and a large wheel. The bow on this wreck is excellent. The masts are broken at seven and twelve feet up from the deck. Our sources want this wreck kept as it is. As a result, we are not able to publish the coordinates of this site.

Towing steamer *Jay Gould*. Authors' Collection

CONSTITUTION

Official #:	4568	**Site #:**	5

Location: Kelleys Island West Bay Dock

Coordinates: GPS: 41 36.504 82 43.752   LORAN: 43677.4 56973.2

Lies: bow northeast   **Depth:** 20 feet

Type: 3 masted schooner   **Cargo:** stone

Power: sail

Owner(s) Runnels and Sinclair of Port Huron, Michigan

Built: 1861 by B.B. Jones at Milwaukee, Wisconsin

Dimensions: 148' x 32' x 12'   **Tonnage:** 422 gross, 401 net

Date of Loss: Thursday, September 20, 1906

Cause of Loss: sprung a leak

Constitution sunk at West Dock

Rutherford B. Hayes Presidential Center, Fremont, Ohio

Story of the Loss:

Prior to World War II, Kelleys Island was a primary source of quarried stone for construction and steel manufacturing.   The *Constitution* was one of many vessels that called on her docks to pick up stone and lime. Visitors to Kelleys Island can see some of this history at the Kelleys Island State Park East Quarry. The main entrance is about a mile east of Division Street on Ward Road. Hikers can also enter the quarry area on Monagan and Woodford Roads. This quarry was part of a much larger quarry to the west of Division Street. The Kelleys Island Lime and Transport Company began quarrying this area around 1933, when they acquired several smaller quarries and linked them with a narrow gauge rail line. This continued until 1940. The quarry stretched from Division Street to the head of Horseshoe Lake. Quarried stone was hauled west on the narrow gauge railway. Some of the tracks of the abandoned rail line still extend beneath Lake Erie's waters. Between the effects of the Great Depression and changes in the building stone trade Kelleys Island Lime & Transport Company was eventually forced to close its quarries. The last loads were shipped just prior to the outbreak of World War II. However, quarrying limestone continues on Kelleys Island. In 2004, La Farge of North America purchased the 200 acre Kellstone Quarry. This quarry still has the capacity to produce more than a million tons of limestone each year. Most is shipped by barge to Cleveland docks where it is sold as construction aggregate.

One of the sad facts of life for wooden sailing vessels is that when the vessel neared the end of its career, there were only a few cargos that could be carried on a leaky boat. The *Constitution* was originally built as a bark with square sails on the forward mast. However, with her rigging changed and at the ripe old age of 45 years old, the *Constitution* was near the end of her career. The leaky old boat was calling at the Kelleys Island Lime and Transportation Company dock on the west side of the island to load limestone. The load filled her holds and was piled high on her decks. This overloading undoubtedly contributed to her descent to the bottom. As the vessel started to settle to the bottom while sitting at the dock, there was no steam to operate her pumps. Having no hope of saving the vessel, the six man crew simply stepped to the safety of the dock as she foundered.

Given her age, the decision was taken not to pump her out and raise her. Rather, she was cleared from the side of the dock and her remains were left for fish to enjoy and for man to forget.

The Wreck Today:

The *Constitution* sits on a rock bottom with her sides splayed open by her stone cargo. The wreck is easily accessible as a shore dive as it sits about 100 feet from shore off the yellow house next to West Dock. Caution is required as boat traffic, both recreational and commercial, and fishing are extremely heavy in this area.

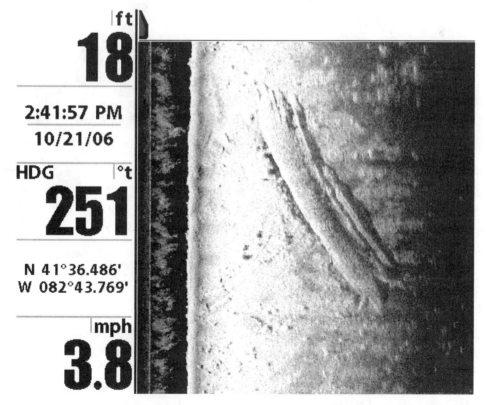

Side scan image of the *Constitution by the authors.*

L.B. CROCKER

Official #:	14710	**Site #:**	6
Location:	west side of Kelleys Island. Ohio		
Coordinates:	GPS: 41 36.443 82 44.428		
Lies:	northeast / southwest	**Depth:**	23 - 25 feet
Type:	schooner barge	**Cargo:**	none
Power:	sail or towed		
Owner(s)	Captain Hoose of Detroit, Michigan		
Built:	1853 at Detroit, Michigan		
Dimensions:	122' to 20.3' x 10'	**Tonnage:**	238.34 gross 226.43 net
Date of Loss:	Sunday, April 20, 1884		
Cause of Loss:	storm		

Canadian tug towing a schooner / barge similar to the L.B. Crocker

Author's Collection

Story of the Loss:

The *L.B. Crocker* had been towed down from Port Huron, Michigan by the Canadian tug *Kittie Haight* to take on a load of stone for the return trip. The *Crocker* was under command of the owner's son, Captain Hoose. Captain Chris Smith, of the *Kittie Haight*, advised young Captain Hoose to anchor away from Kelleys Island in case a storm came up. Unfortunately, Captain Hoose chose to anchor close to Carpenter's Point, which is on the west side of the island, near the stone docks. A gale did indeed blow through the area in the night, and the *Crocker* was driven so close to the beach, that the crew had only to put out a plank and "walk it" to shore.

Because the island had a couple of limestone quarries, Kelleys Island was the last port of call for numerous vessels on Lake Erie. Whenever a vessel could no longer be insured to carry grain (a cargo that had to be kept dry) the boat would switch to carrying coal, and finally stone. A rock cargo was considered undesirable by the crew as it often had to be wheeled on by hand and overloading was a common practice. Deck loads often made handling lines difficult and seafaring very dangerous in the aging, leaky vessels to which the task usually fell.

Stone to be loaded on the *L.B Crocker* was quarried in the nearby island quarries. Authors' collection

By Tuesday, the passing steamer *Alaska* reported that the *Crocker* was breaking up. This was not surprising. The thirty year old vessel was in such poor shape that the *Inland Lloyds Register* of insurance rated her zero. However, the newspapers said she could be worth as much as $1,800. By Wednesday, she had been stripped and abandoned.

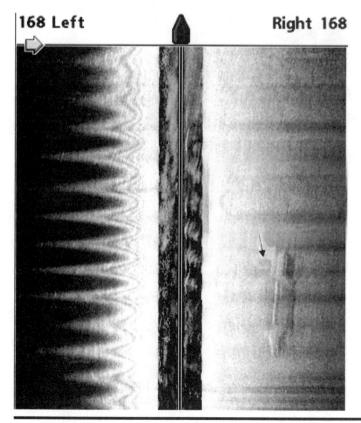

The Wreck Today:

The piece of the hull in our side scan image appears to be over 100 feet long. However, we did not have an opportunity to dive this wreck. There were several vessels wrecked on the west side of Kelleys Island. These include the *Oak Valley*, 22.5 tons sunk in 1882, the *L.B. Crocker*, and the tug *Relief* that was destroyed by fire and then towed from Starve Island to Kelleys Island in July of 1884.

Based on her size and location, we suspect this target is the *L.B. Crocker*. However, it will require additional investigation to rule out other possibilities, including the *Relief*, which is covered in *Erie Wrecks West*.

Side scan image by the authors.

CSU Wreck

Official #:	unknown	**Site #:**	21
Location:	2.3 miles, 8°T from the entrance to Cleveland Harbor, Ohio		
Coordinates:	GPS: 41 32.604 81 42.617		
Lies:	bow northwest	**Depth:**	45 feet
Type:	wooden tug or barge	**Cargo:**	unknown
Power:	unknown		
Owner(s)	unknown		
Built:	unknown		
Dimensions:	approximately 90 feet long	**Tonnage:**	unknown
Date of Loss:	after 1900		
Cause of Loss:	unknown		

Diver examines crockery on CSU Wreck.

Photo by Georgann Wachter

Story of the Loss:

Unknown

The Wreck Today:

This little wreck lies on its port side most of which, is either missing or buried. At the bow is a tow bit and hatch. She is called the *CSU Wreck* because her true identity is unknown, and she sits off of Cleveland State University's Main Classroom Building on Cleveland's near east side.

For a beaten up wreck site, there is a lot to see. This vessel is double planked with some metal sheeting on the hull. Deck caulking is evident. There are pegs to seal nail holes, and metal fasteners are driven into the deck. At the stern, there is a six foot triangular pieces of metal of unknown function. There is some evidence that this vessel may have burned. Around the wreck, one can find many bricks, clinkers, and some coal strewn across the sand bottom.

What really makes this site interesting is the amount of crockery scattered about. This suggests this vessel was not scuttled, but sank due to unintentional circumstances. We found a blue edged plate, one intact brown jug, a couple of broken crocks, plus parts of other plates. One plate is marked "SCC Akron, Ohio".

The Summit China Company of Akron, Ohio (SCC Akron, Ohio) began business in 1901 and continued production until sometime after 1929. As such, the pottery gives us an indication of when the *CSU Wreck* met her demise.

While we do not yet have enough information to put a proper name to this shipwreck, we anticipate additional research and site investigation can get her to give up her secret.

CAUTION: Due to its proximity to Cleveland Harbor, this site has heavy recreational and commercial boat traffic.

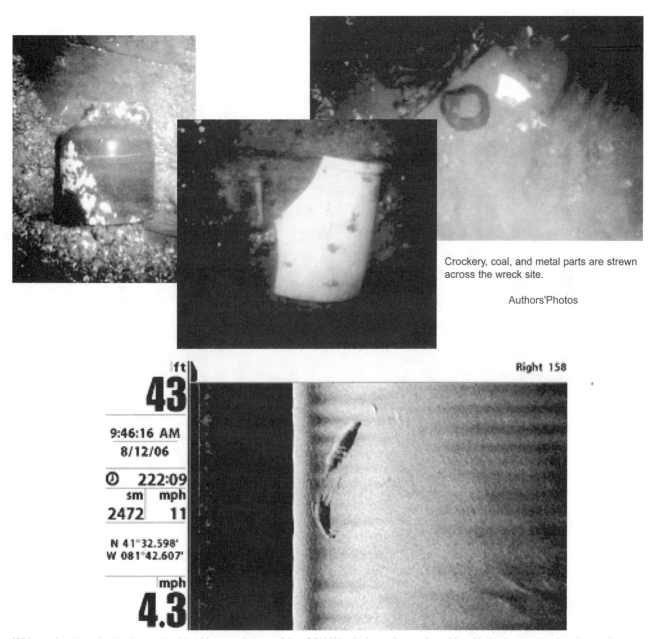

Crockery, coal, and metal parts are strewn across the wreck site.

Authors'Photos

With our boat headed to the south, this side scan image of the *CSU Wreck* shows her on her side with the bow pointed to the northwest.
Side scan imagery by the authors.

CUSTODIAN

Official #: 218783   **Site #:**   1

Location: east side of West Sister Island, tucked in on the north side of the sand spit

Coordinates: GPS: 41 44. 263 83 06.149

Lies: scattered   **Depth:**   12 feet

Type: wooden tug   **Cargo:**   not applicable

Power: steam propeller with two boilers and triple expansion 18", 28", 45" cylinders with a 30 inch stroke.

Owner(s) Pringle Barge Line, Cleveland, Ohio

Built: 1919 for the U.S. Navy by M.M. Davis & Sons at Solomons Island, Maryland

Dimensions: 126' x 29.9' x 13.7'   **Tonnage:** 359 gross   199 net

Date of Loss: Tuesday, June 23, 1925

Cause of Loss: burned

Custodian

Private Collection of Ralph Roberts

Story of the Loss:

The tug *Custodian* was towing the barge *Madia* when she caught fire at 10 in the evening. Captain Henry (Hank) C. Buchsiet of Toledo reported that the tug was enveloped in flames of unknown origin so quickly that his men lost their clothes. In fact, the members of the crew left the tug before the engine was stopped. They were picked up by the *Madia* which, in turn, was taken in tow by the tug *Guardian* the following day. All were safely landed in Cleveland, Ohio. Some marine men in the Toledo tug office swore Captain Hank set fire to her. The boilers were salvaged and eventually used in a Toledo greenhouse.

In 1937, West Sister Island was declared a "refuge and breeding ground for migratory birds and other wildlife" by President Franklin Delano Roosevelt. Seventy seven of the islands 82 acres were designated a federal wilderness area in 1975. Today, it is considered to be the largest wading bird nesting colony on the U.S. Great Lakes. West Sister Island National Wildlife Refuge is jointly owned by the U.S. Fish and Wildlife Service and the U.S. Coast Guard. The preserve is managed by the Ottawa National Wildlife Refuge as a wilderness area. As of this writing, West Sister Island is Ohio's only wilderness area.

In a not so well known historical fact, West Sister Island first made its reputation in history during the War of 1812. On September 10, 1813, Commodore Oliver Hazard Perry sent an immortal message to General William Harrison from West Sister Island after the Battle of Lake Erie. The message read, "We have met the enemy, and they are ours, two ships, two brigs, one schooner and one sloop."

The first lighthouse was constructed on West Sister Island in 1821. The current lighthouse replaced it in 1847. Lighthouse keepers lived on the island with their families until the light was automated in 1937. The only building remaining on the island today is the aging 55-foot tall lighthouse.

The Wreck Today:

During World War II, starting in April 1945, the War Department bombed the island to test stadiametric aircraft gunsights. Targets included not only the island, but also the tug *Custodian*, a cabin cruiser, and the lighthouse. Although the island has not been used for military purposes since 1951, there may still be ordinance in the area, which should be considered unstable and explosive. It has also been reported that fuel tanks, jettisoned by dive bombers, have been found on the island.

The rocky outcrop on the southeast side of West Sister extends quite a way out. It is wise to approach from the north. The remains of the tug are only about 50 feet off the rocky cliff, and they have the potential to be a propeller bender since there is only five feet or less clearance over the wreck.

For a shallow water site, there is quite a bit left of this wreck. Among the debris, lying flat on the rock bottom, is a large rudder with brass straps. Part of the cabin cruiser's engine also rests nearby.

NOTICE: To protect this wilderness nesting area, public access to the island is only permitted for research.

The *Custodian* rests near the rock shore just north of the rocky outcropping on the southeast side of West Sister Island.
Photo by the authors.

DETROITER

Official #: none   **Site #:** 4

Location: 2.9 miles at 7° T from the entrance to the Portage River

Coordinates: GPS: 41 33.663 82 55.744   LORAN: 43628.5 56858.0

Lies: bow south   **Depth:** 20 feet

Type: steam dredge barge   **Cargo:** not applicable

Power: two steam maneuvering engines

Owner(s) Bay City Construction

Built: before 1929

Dimensions: 60′ x 32′ x 4′   **Tonnage:** 359 gross   199 net

Date of Loss: early to mid 1980s

Cause of Loss: storm

Bay Bridge Construction

Great Lakes Historical Society photo

Story of the Loss:

This stiff legged steam barge had the distinction of being used by Bentley Construction of Toledo, Ohio to build the original Sandusky Bay Bridge, completed in 1929. In 1926 the State of Ohio rerouted State Route 2 along the southern shore of Lake Erie between Toledo and Cleveland. The only problem was the barrier created by Sandusky Bay, which lies between Sandusky and the Marblehead Peninsula. To travel around the bay by land required a 40-mile trip southwest to Fremont and then back northeast to Sandusky. The only direct routes across the bay were a regular ferry service from Bay Point and downtown Sandusky, and the New York Central Railroad Bridge that connected the two sides. This condition was alleviated when, in 1929, the Sandusky Bay Bridge Company opened the first automobile bridge to cross the bay. This original bridge was a half mile long drawbridge with mile long causeways connecting it to the northern and southern banks of the bay. Privately owned and requiring a toll to cross, the bridge carried Ohio Route 2 across the bay until it was closed in 1984. The two causeways are still maintained for fishing and recreation. The causeways can be accessed from exits on either end of the modern day Edison Bridge.

The *Detroiter* was sold to David B. Jeremy & Sons around 1945. The *Detroiter* worked on many western Lake Erie projects, including: the Newman Dock at Kelleys Island, the Lime Kiln Dock at South Bass Island, and the Lakeside fishing piers in the 1940s. She was sold to Bay City Construction and her boiler, derrick, and steam slewing engine were removed. The new owners were towing her from Port Clinton, Ohio to Detroit, Michigan when a storm developed. As the tugs pushed her into a head sea, her hatches blew, and she was lost near Middle Sister Island. In a botched salvage attempt, she was raised and moved to her current location.

The Wreck Today:

Located on a mud bottom near the east end of the Camp Perry Firing Range, her large winch is only about 12 feet below the water's surface. The barge lies on a north/south axis with a large hand worked anchor off of the wreck. To the east is coiled cable and a debris field. To the south is what we believe to be a smoke stack. One spud remains on the southwest corner and bollard style tow bit is at the bow.

CAUTION: As this wreck sits in close proximity to Camp Perry's Firing Range, you should heed the marine radio warning broadcast on channel 16 when there is firing in the nearby impact area to the north and west.

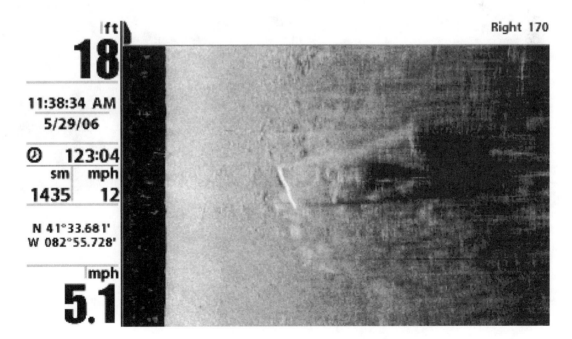

Side scan image of the *Detroiter* by the authors

Esco #2

Official #:   was US 176677   **Site #:**   24

Location: 8.7 miles at 55° T off the entrance to Fairport Harbor - two miles off Perry, Ohio

Coordinates: GPS: 41 50.345   81 08.467   LORAN: 44024.8 57861.6

Lies: bow west   **Depth:**   55 feet

Type: dredge barge   **Cargo:**   none

Power: towed

Owner(s)   Marine Salvage, Ltd, Port Colborne, Ontario

Built: 1924 at Rochester, Pennsylvania

Dimensions: 101.5' x 34' x 5.6'   **Tonnage:**   267 gross   267 net

Date of Loss: Monday, September 14, 1970

Cause of Loss: sprug a leak

Esco #2

Photo courtesy of Harry Goodman

Story of the Loss:

Originally, this barge was built for the Army Corps of Engineers as the *Allegheny*. During her long life as the *King Coal*, this sturdy barge participated in many construction projects. Her fourth owner, for 11 years, was the L.A. Wells Construction Company. Her tasks with the Wells Company included dredging at Erie and Conneaut, creation of coal docks in Huron, water intakes at Avon Lake and Rocky River, and construction of Sandusky's Cedar Point Causeway. The causeway was opened on June 12, 1959, providing, for the first time, an easily accessible route to the Lake Erie peninsula and stimulating the development of the second oldest amusement park in the world. That park is now the world's number one rated amusement park, Cedar Point.

By 1970, the 46 year old barge had seen better days. The often patched *King Coal* had sunk earlier off of Avon Lake, Ohio. Having now outlived her usefulness, she was renamed *Esco #2*, and sold to Canadian Marine Salvage for scrapping in Port Colborne, Ontario. She departed Cleveland, Ohio behind the tug *Herbert A* in the company of the derrick scow *Aft*. The *Aft* was also scheduled to be broken up for scrap. During the night, as they were off Fairport, the tug and her consorts encountered high waves. The *Esco*

King Coal working on the Cedar Point Causeway.
Photo courtesy of Harry Goodman

#2 began sinking. The *Herbert A* abandoned her west of Fairport Harbor and continued on to Port Colborne with the *Aft* still in tow. The *Esco #2* drifted several miles east before sinking off of Perry, Ohio.

Aft Barge and *King Coal* ready for towing
Photo courtesy of Harry Goodman

The Wreck Today:

Located in about 45 feet of water, the *Esco #2* is three quarters turtled. Her south side opens up about 9 feet off the bottom. The trench surrounding the wreck reaches 55 feet deep. Part of the deck house can be found off to the east and south of the hull. You can see the large holes in the southwest end where the spuds were torn out. Cable, chain, and tires are suspended from her red, black, and white hull. There are concrete patched holes evident across her bottom.

GOLD COAST TUG

Official #:   **Site #:**   17

Location: 3.0 miles at 277° T off the main Cleveland, Ohio Harbor entrance

Coordinates: GPS: 41 30.916   81 46.535

Lies: bow west   **Depth:**   45 feet

Type: wood tug   **Cargo:**   none

Power: steam as a working tug, towed when scuttled

Owner(s)   Great Lakes Towing Company, Cleveland, Ohio

Built: unknown

Dimensions: unknown   **Tonnage:** unknown

Date of Loss: Between 1903 and 1916

Cause of Loss: scuttled

Great Lakes Towing Company Tugs on the Buffalo River

Postcard courtesy of Al Hart

Story of the Wreck

In the early 1900s the Great Lakes Towing Company found themselves with several vessels that needed upgrading. Between 1903 and 1916 at least eight tugs were stripped of various parts and then taken out in the lake and scuttled. The sixty-eight foot long tug *George R. Paige* was sunk in 1903, the *J.C. Evans* in 1914, the tugs *Joe Harris*, *Chicago*, *William L. Scott*, and *W.I. Babcock* went to the bottom in 1915. And, the *Robert H. Herbard* was sunk in 1916.

We are not sure which of these tugs is at this site. However, among those scuttled was the seventy-one foot *W.I. Babcock*, which was built in 1888 at Buffalo, New York. The postcard on the previous page shows her at Buffalo. The *J.C. Evans* was built in 1876 in Milwaukee. The postcard to the right shows her at Chicago.

The Wreck Today

We nicknamed this tug the *Gold Coast Tug* because it rests off a series of high rise residences in Lakewood, Ohio which bear the same moniker.

Today this tug is buried in the mud except for her boiler and condenser. A short distance east is her steel rudder. Divers should watch for heavy boat traffic, including sailboat races. For information on other tugs in the area, see the *M.F. Merick* and *Lakewood Tug* in this volume and the *117th Street Wreck* in *Erie Wrecks West*.

J.C. Evans at Chicago
Postcard collection of Al Hart

The *Gold Coast Tug* and other scuttled tugs all sit off of the Lakewood Gold Coast high rise apartments. Cleveland Harbor is in the background.
Photo by authors.

HAMMERMILL WRECK

Official #:   **Site #:**   30
Location: 0.69 miles at 172° T off the Erie Harbor Pierhead Light
Coordinates: GPS: 42 08.767   80 04.147
Lies: broken up and scattered   **Depth:**   8 feet
Type: unknown   **Cargo:**
Power: unknown
Owner(s)   unknown
Built: unknown
Dimensions: unknown   **Tonnage:** unknown
Date of Loss: unknown
Cause of Loss: possibly scuttled

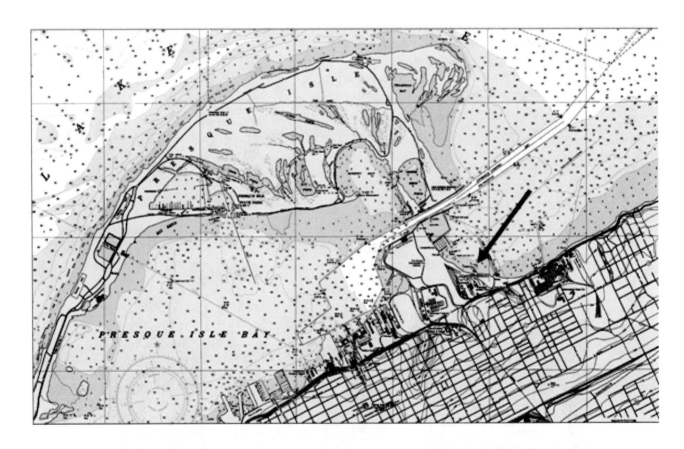

The location of the *Hammermill Wreck* makes it difficult to access by boat without creating another wreck site.

Story of the Wreck

This wreck is named for the Hammermill Paper Plant located about one half mile to the east of the site.

The Wreck Today:

This broken up and partially burned shipwreck is located south of the Lampe Marina. Since directions to the site include "going across the large rock" one would guess that this would be a shore dive. If you do choose to take a boat be sure it has a very shallow draft. The intake crib to the west of the site has only one foot of water over it, and there is a submerged pier to the east.

The calm waters of the Erie Harbor entrance channel lie immediately north of the *Hammermill Wreck* and are watched over by the Erie Pierhead Light and the Brig Niagara seen sailing in the distance.
Photo by Georgann Wachter.

Rescuers from the Erie Life Saving Station undoubtedly went to the aid of the *Hammermill Wreck*. Photo from U.S. Coast Guard Station Erie scrapbooks.

INTERNATIONAL

Official #:	12070	**Site #:**	38
Location:	4/10 mile below the Peace Bridge at Fort Erie, Ontario		
Coordinates:	GPS: PA 42 54.200 78 54.935		
Lies:	bow north northeast	**Depth:**	10 feet
Type:	sidewheel steamer	**Cargo:**	none
Power:	two low pressure horizontal engines - 42" cylinders with 9' stroke		
Owner(s)	Buffalo and Lake Huron Railroad (Great Western Railroad)		
Built:	1857 at Buffalo, New York by Bidwell and Banta Company		
Dimensions:	220' x 40.2' x 11.2'	**Tonnage:**	1135 gross
Date of Loss:	Monday, February 2, 1874		
Cause of Loss:	fire		

FORT ERIE, ONTARIO, SEPTEMBER 13, 1962

The Times-Review

RAILWAY FERRY In the eventful pages of Fort Erie history is the old ferry that transported railway cars across the Niagara River in the early 1800's. It was in operation until about 1870, and was discontinued when the International Railway Bridge was opened in 1872. The old railway grade on Albany street off the Garrison road can still be seen although the pier is gone. The ferry docked just south of the "old mill race" and old-timers will recall where that was, it was near where No. 3

Highway adjoins Niagara boulevard. The terminal on the east side of the river was near old Fort Porter. The Times-Review appreciates the kindness of Mrs. Henry Warren Lewis, 479 Niagara boulevard, and Bert Miller, 97 Butte street, in providing the fine photograph and the very interesting information on the ferry. The photographer's work must have been excellent for the depth of the scene to reproduce so well after all these years.

Photo Courtesy Mrs. Lewis

International

Photo from *The Times Review*

Story of the Wreck

The *International* was the first railroad carferry to operate on the Great Lakes. She was the successor of a passenger ferry of the same name that was destroyed by fire at her wharf in Buffalo in December of 1854.

The ferry's capacity was 8 passenger coaches or freight cars carried on tracks that were standard 5'6" for Canadian gauge cars. Additional tracks were laid down in Buffalo to admit United States gauge (4'8½") cars. Passengers would board in Canadian cities and arrive in Buffalo without leaving their coaches. It was only a fifteen minute ride across the Niagara River.

In fact, the ferry often made excursions to Niagara Falls. In 1866 the teachers and pupils of Buffalo Public School Number 15 went on a picnic to Niagara, crossing on the *International* to see the "beautiful scenery" by train. The cost was seventy-five cents.

From its inception, the Buffalo and Lake Huron Railroad had planned the eventual construction of a bridge to link the two countries. As a result, the *International* was designed to be converted to a freight vessel. She had a two deck high shed, which was open at either end, to stow the railroad cars. In 1872, the tracks on the ferry were altered to a standard 4'8½" gauge.

On November 3, 1873, the rail bridge International was opened. This made the carferry *International* obsolete, and she was tied up at her Fort Erie, Ontario wharf. The fire that destroyed her was first noticed at 9:45pm, but it was not until 11:15pm that a resident across the Niagara River reported the conflagration. It was believed that the fire that burned her to the waterline was deliberately set.

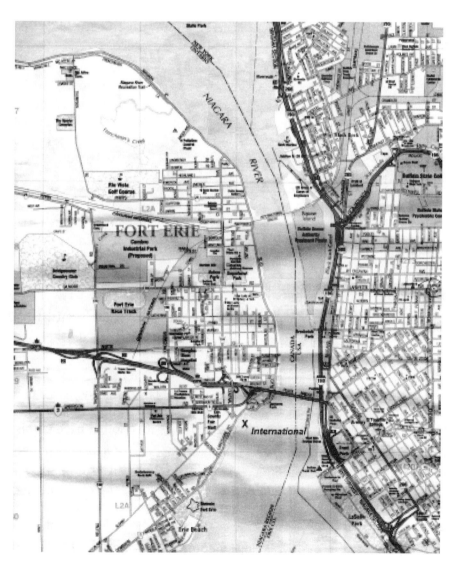

The Wreck Today

The *International* sits alongside the remains of her Canadian ferry dock in Fort Erie. The dock was off Lakeshore Road Park, which runs under the current Peace Bridge. The keel of the *International* still sits on the rocky bottom. A swift current is apparently undermining the rocks that had supported the dock, partially covering the wreck.

Look for her burned timbers, and watch for boats and current at this shallow water site.

KING COAL

Official #:	was US 176677	**Site #:**	15
Location:	1/4 mile off Avon Lake, Ohio		
Coordinates:	GPS: 41 30.626 82 02.833		
Lies:	mostly removed	**Depth:**	15 feet
Type:	steam powered dredge barge	**Cargo:**	none
Power:	towed		
Owner(s)	Esco Dredge and Fill Corporation of Erie, Pennsylvania		
Built:	1924 at Rochester, Pennsylvania		
Dimensions:	101.5 x 34 x 5.6	**Tonnage:**	267 gross
Date of Loss:	Wednesday, June14, 1961		
Cause of Loss:	storm		

King Coal with Avon Lake Power Plant in the background

Photo from private collection of Ralph Roberts

Story of the Loss:

The *King Coal* was built for the US Army Corp of Engineers and was named *Allegheny* until 1946. Her next owner, Rivercoal Inc. of Wheeling, West Virginia, dubbed her *King Coal*. This moniker stuck until just before her final loss. But that is another story for another page of this book (check out *Esco #2*).

For nine years, the L.A. Wells Construction Company of Cleveland, Ohio owned this vessel. Wells Construction did numerous projects around the Great Lakes -- installing docks, breakwaters, and water intakes. The company had won the contract for installation of a water intake at Avon Lake, Ohio. However, Louis Wells had decided to retire. To facilitate this, he sold the Avon Lake contract and most of his equipment to the Esco Dredge & Fill Corporation of Erie, Pennsylvania.

On June 14 of 1961, while installing the water intake, *King Coal* was caught in a sudden storm. When the wind came up, the bargemen had been trenching in 12 feet of water. The *King Coal's* dredge bucket caught on something beneath the water and anchored the barge to the bottom in seas that would soon build to ten feet high. Their tug, the *Stella B*, was able to rescue four of the men from the barge before a cable fouled her propeller. She set her anchor but it did not hold. The tug was cast onto the shore in front of the Cleveland Electric Illuminating Plant. A crane operator on shore, Floyd Morrow, was able to lower his giant shovel to pluck 6 men, two at a time, form the stranded tug. While this was going on one crewman, James Williamson, remained on the sinking *King Coal*. He was rescued from the cabin top by the a vessel out of Coast Guard Station Cleveland just as the *King Coal* settled to the bottom of the lake.

Crane Plucks 8 Men From Peril on Storm-Tossed Lake Barge

PRESS JUNE 14, 1961

An ill wind blew some good for eight men drifting in stormy Lake Erie off Avon Lake this afternoon.

After tossing them around for more than an hour, the wind finally blew them into shore to safety.

A crane operator working nearby plucked them out of the lake with his sand bucket, two men at a time.

The rescued men all are employees of the Esco Dredge and Fill Co. They were working on a new water intake directly out into the lake from the Illuminating Co. plant.

Six of the men were working on a 40-foot barge. Two were on a tug, the B-Stella, which was towing the barge.

Suddenly the crane on the barge broke and the barge began to sink.

The tug started to tow the barge into shore when the cable snapped and wound around the screws, fouling the motor.

By this time the winds were whipping up and both vessels began to toss helplessly.

Then the wind began to do some good. It blew the tug close enough to the barge so that the six workmen could jump from the sinking barge to the tug. Two men were on the tug.

Watching the action from shore—about 200 yards away—was Floyd Morrow, 3° of

Columbia Station. He was operating a crane behind the CEI plant. He began rounding up life jackets and search for rescue workers.

Then the wind blew the tug close enough to shore for Morrow to jockey his crane onto a narrow point of land from which he picked the men up in his bucket a pair at a time.

The men were wet and weary, but in good condition.

They were immediately sent to their homes for recuperation. Some of their names, listed by the Illuminating Co., are H. Bourque, E. McCoy, J. Wintringham, Williamson, Robert Mariner, S. Conroy and Cheesman.

Article from the *Cleveland Press*, June 14, 1961

The Wreck Today:

The General Manager of ESCO supervised the salvage of both vessels. However, not all of the *King Coal* was recovered. In a gravel filled trench, remains from the *King Coal's* first encounter with the bottom of Lake Erie can still be found. There are metal pieces of the barge's house, acetylene tanks, and cable. To the east on the rocky bottom is a 25 foot long spud and six foot bracing that was abandoned on the bottom following the salvage.

First encounter with the bottom, you ask? Yes, this was not to be the *King Coal's* last trip to the bottom of Lake Erie. For her final chapter, see the *Esco #2*.

Crane operator Floyd Morrow rescues crew from tug.
King Coal can be seen sunk in the background.
Photo from June 14, 1961, *Cleveland Press*

LAKEWOOD TUG

Official #:   **Site #:**   19

Location: 2.8 miles at 285° T from the Cleveland Harbor Main Entrance

Coordinates: GPS: 41 31.178   81 46.135

Lies: bow northeast   **Depth:**   45 feet

Type: tug   **Cargo:**   none

Power: steam

Owner(s)   Great Lakes Towing Company, Cleveland, Ohio

Built:

Dimensions: unknown   **Tonnage:** 267 gross

Date of Loss: between 1903 and 1916

Cause of Loss: scuttled

Tug ready to be scuttled

Photo from Authors' Collection

Story of the Loss:

We do not know which of the scuttled Great Lakes Towing Company tugs is at this site. However, among the eight tugs deliberately sent to the bottom was the *Joe Harris*.

The wooden harbor tug *Joe Harris* was one of the tugs scuttled by her last owner, the Great Lakes Towing Company. She had official number 75513 and was built in Cleveland by Thomas Quayle. The tug's dimensions were 72.5' x 17.5' x 10', and she was 66 gross tons. The *Joe Harris'* hull was scrapped in 1915.

Eastland under tow by the tug *Joe Harris*. From collection of Al Hart

In the postcard, she is shown towing the infamous steamer *Eastland*. Beginning in 1908, the *Eastland* carried passengers on the Cleveland - Cedar Point - Sandusky run. In 1913, the *Eastland* returned to her original home port of Chicago. On July 24, 1915, the steamer, docked on the Chicago River, had boarded excursionist from the Western Electric Company. As she let go her lines, the ship rolled over. Approximately 835 people were drowned in the incident. This is the worst loss of life disaster in the history of the Great Lakes.

The Wreck Today:

When diving the mud bottom off of Lakewood, Ohio be careful of the heavy boat traffic in the area. Traffic includes sailboat races from nearby marinas. The tug lays hard over on its side and one gunnel is buried in the bottom of the lake. Visibility is often poor at this site. Nearby are the remains of the other scuttled tugs. These include the *M.F. Merick,* the *Gold Coast Tug,* and the *117th Street Wreck.*

Side scan image of the *Lakewood Tug*

Official #:	n/a		**Site #:**	35
Location:	4.6 miles west of Port Maitland, off Low Point			
Coordinates:	GPS: 42 50.152 79 40.074 LORAN: 44736.0 58832.5			
Lies:	scattered		**Depth:**	10 to 15 feet
Type:	railroad cars		**Cargo:**	steel and coal
Power:	towed			
Owner(s)	Toronto, Hamilton and Buffalo Navigation Company			
Built:				
Dimensions:			**Tonnage:**	
Date of Loss:	Tuesday, December 23, 1919			
Cause of Loss:	stranding			

Maitland No.1

Jim Smith Photo

Story of the Loss:

Several railroad carferries operated for extended seasons linking rail lines in the US and Canada. These carferries shortened the land trip by many miles and often carried more than 30 rail cars. Common cargos were coal and steel. Most were operated by the Pere Marquette Railroad Company. One small line was operated by TH&B. The TH&B (Toronto, Hamilton & Buffalo Railway) existed from 1892 through 1987 as a separate railway serving the Hamilton, Ontario area. It was established to provide an alternate route for businesses in the Hamilton area to ship their products to Canadian customers in Toronto, Montreal, and the west, and to American customers via the New York Central and its subsidiaries. After July 1895, the TH&B was jointly owned by the Canadian Provincial Railway Company and the New York Central Railroad (and its successor, Penn Central). In 1977 CP Rail bought the remaining shares and became full owner of the railway. In 1987, the TH&B was integrated into the operations of its parent and lost its distinct identity as a separate railway. This railway owned a subsidiary company, the TH&B Navigation Company, to operate a rail ferry. Chartered in 1916, TH&B Navigation Company operated the *Maitland No.1*, which plied the waters between Ashtabula, Ohio and Port Maitland, Ontario until 1932.

Marquette and Bessemer No.1 helped pull the *Maitland* off Low Point.

During her career, the *Maitland* had two serious groundings. The second was on March 25, 1927. On that occasion, fog and heavy ice were blamed when she stranded on Tecumseh Reef and damaged 18 of her hull plates. The tug *Thompson* pulled her off a day later, but sunk herself in the process. There are reports that some rail cars were jettisoned at that time in order to lighten the vessel sufficiently to permit her to be refloated. However, based on their location, an earlier grounding is probably the source of the railroad debris off Low Point.

On December 23, 1919, the *Maitland* was carrying 26 rail cars when she grounded on Low Point. The Great Lakes Towing Company tugs *Texas* and *Tennessee* left Buffalo, New York on Christmas eve to attempt the salvage of the *Maitland No.1*. They were joined by the carferry *Ashtabula*. Stuck fast in 11 to 16 feet of water, the *Maitland* was a good three feet out of the water. All three vessels pulled on the stranded carferry for four hours on Christmas day. Their efforts were to no avail. As heavy weather set in, concern was raised that the *Maitland No.1* would be irreparably damaged. Two more tugs, the *Vermont* and *New York*, and the collier *Marquette and Bessemer* No.1 were diverted to the scene from other parts of the lake. Even with the enormous towing power of four tugs and two steamers the *Maitland No.1*

Ice covered carferry loaded with rail cars.

would not budge. It was not until seven cars of coal and one car of steel were dumped that the *Maitland* could "enjoy" a belated Christmas and a huge salvage bill.

Although the *Maitland* did not suffer too much damage in this stranding, Captain John Keeley was suspended for 10 days for failure to order soundings and slack speed.

The Wreck Today:

This shallow water site offers three metal and two wood railroad cars. In addition, there are wheel trucks and steel cargo is widely spread across the bottom. Try not to impale your boat on the reef.

MAUTENEE

Official #:	50962	**Site #:**	32
Location:	18 miles east of Erie, Pennsylvania		
Coordinates:	GPS: PA 42 17.115 79 43.200		
Lies:	bow northwest	**Depth:**	10 feet
Type:	schooner / barge	**Cargo:**	none
Power:	sail		
Owner(s)	Thomas F. Madden of Bay City Michigan		
Built:	1873 at Trenton, Michigan by Maxwell Turner		
Dimensions:	200' x 34' x 14.8'	**Tonnage:**	647
Date of Loss:	Friday, October 20, 1905		
Cause of Loss:	storm		

Wreck of the Mautenee, Oct. 20/05, Ripley, N. Y.

Mautenee

Authors' Collection

Story of the Loss:

A massive storm that devastated Lakes Michigan, Huron, and Erie was the demise of the schooner barge *Mautenee*. The barge was 212 feet length overall and had been built as a three sticker. She had one mast and her topmasts removed to facilitate her conversion to a towed barge. A pony boiler mounted forward powered her windlass and loading machinery.

The *Mautenee* was under tow on a voyage from Buffalo to Duluth. As she traveled through worsening weather, she was either cut loose or broke loose from her tow. She was pushed before waves on a lake described as, "such a sea has not been experienced by sailors on the lakes in the last fifteen years. Many of the largest barges, which make nothing of usually heavy seas this time of year, were compelled to seek shelter at the nearest ports." (*The Evening News* of Buffalo, October 21, 1905)

Master Thomas Madden had his crew deploy both anchors, but the schooner continued to drift toward the New York shore. Once on the beach, the three decade old vessel began to be torn asunder by the roaring surf. Finding it impossible to launch the lifeboat, the crew was in imminent danger in the mountainous seas. Fortunately, one crewman volunteered to swim a line to shore. While this sailor almost perished in his attempt to get the hawser to the beach, he was successful in getting the line ashore and attaching it securely.

The balance of the crew, including the cook, Mrs. Katy Daly, came ashore on a breaches buoy. The *Mautenee* was abandoned and allowed to break up on shore.

The Wreck Today:

At least one anchor from the *Mautenee* was removed. It rests in a yard at Findley Lake, New York. Although some of her timber was salvaged, parts of the keel and frames are spread across this shallow water site on the rock and sand bottom.

Breeches buoy rescue.

M.F. Merick

Official #:	90492	**Site #:**	18
Location:	3 miles at 285° T from Cleveland Harbor's main entrance		
Coordinates:	GPS: 41 31.227 81 46.317		
Lies:	bow west	**Depth:**	45 feet
Type:	wooden tug	**Cargo:**	not applicable
Power:	steam engine with double 20" x 24' cylinders		
Owner(s)	Great Lakes Towing Company, Cleveland, Ohio		
Built:	1873 by Detroit Dry Dock Company at Detroit, Michigan		
Dimensions:	92' x 24.5' x 10.2'	**Tonnage:**	133 gross
Date of Loss:	circa 1908		
Cause of Loss:	scuttled		

M.F. Merick

Collection of Al Hart

Story of the Loss:

Many years ago, we met some friends out on the lake after their son's wedding. It was a lovely, calm, September day so we decided to see what was on the bottom of the lake.   We dropped down beneath the surface and, much to our surprise, discovered a shipwreck sitting on the bottom. We were sitting off of Lakewood, Ohio in the vicinity of 117th Street. As a result, we assumed that we had found what the old timers called the *117th Street Wreck*. That is how we listed it in our first book, ***Erie Wrecks***. Some years later, one of the old timers was describing "their" *117th Street Wreck* to us and commented on the large boiler on the wreck. "Our" *117th Street Wreck* did not have a boiler. This led us to believe that there had to be more than one wreck in that area.

In 2006, we conducted a side scan search of the area and discovered not one more, but four sets of wreck remains. In the early 1900s the Great Lakes Towing Company of Cleveland disposed of several tugs by stripping them of salvageable items, and then intentionally scuttling them in Lake Erie. In 1903 one tug was scuttled, 1908 another tug, 1914 yet another was sent to the bottom, and in 1915 four hulls were dismantled. The last record we find for any intentional scuttling was 1916, when the *Robert H. Hebard* was stripped of her engine and plopped on the bottom.

Most of these tugs were 60 to 70 feet long. However, the hull at this location measures 90 feet in length. As a result, we believe it to be the *M.F. Merick*. The *Merick* was dismantled in 1907 and briefly used as a lighter. The engine from the tug was put in the tug *L.C. Sabin* in 1908. In 1941 the *L.C. Sabin* was re-named *North Carolina*. As the *North Carolina*, she sank off of Mentor, Ohio in December of 1968.

Though we have located four tugs in this area, we have been told that there are at least two more to be found. See the *Gold Coast Tug* and *Lakewood Tug* in this volume and see the *117th Street Wreck* in *Erie Wrecks West*.

The Wreck Today:

The wooden hull contains metal sheeting at the bow that would have helped reinforce it for towing and ice breaking. There is a list to port, and this side of the tug is either missing or buried. A large 8 foot high boiler is amidships and has two fireboxes. There is no rudder or shaft. However, behind the boiler are four stone blocks that aided her descent to the lake floor. In front of the boiler is a metal mount that probably served to support the now missing engine. The stern rises about six feet off the bottom.

Divers should expect challenged visibility of 6 to 15 feet (we had about 12 feet). One must also watch out for heavy boat traffic and even sailboat races at this site. Sailors out of the Cleveland clubs set one of their turning marks very near this location.

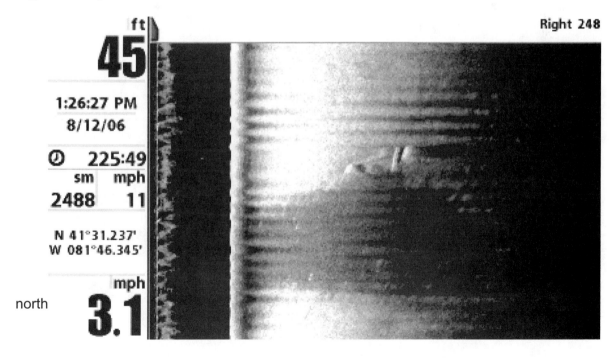

Side scan image of the tug *Merick*. This scan was taken running eastbound. You can clearly see the bow to the west and her boiler in the center of the image. Side scan image by the authors.

BELLE MITCHELL

Official #: 2892   **Site #:** 27

Location: between Conneaut, Ohio and the base of Long Point Peninsula.

Coordinates: still secret

Lies: bow north   **Depth:** 70 feet

Type: two masted schooner   **Cargo:** wheat

Power: gaff rigged sails

Owner(s) A.F. Barker, Captain T.G. Rusho & Mrs. Lettie Grant of Clayton, New York

Built: 1874 by James Navagh at Algonac, Michigan

Dimensions: 136.7' x 25.6' x 11.4'   **Tonnage:** 320 gross   304 net

Date of Loss: Thursday, October 14, 1886

Cause of Loss: storm

Oliver Mitchell sister ship to the Belle

C. Patrick Labadie Collection at Great Lakes Maritime Heritage Center

Story of the Loss:

In 1874, the *Belle Mitchell* and her sister ship the *Oliver Mitchell* were built in Algonac, Michigan by master carpenter James Navagh. They were owned by E. & O. (Edward and Oliver) Mitchell Company, which did business as a cooperage, wheat dealership, and ship building firm operating out of Oswego, New York. The *Belle* was named for Edward's second daughter.

The *Belle Mitchell* had loaded copper on the upper Great Lakes, which was dropped at Sandusky, Ohio. She then proceeded west to Toledo, to load wheat for Buffalo, New York. She left Toledo on Wednesday afternoon the thirteenth. This proved to be an unlucky departure date. By noon on Thursday, a nasty gale was blowing between 30 and 40 miles per hour. The winds increased in the evening to some 55 to 65 m.p.h. out of the southwest. This wind was a remnant of a Gulf hurricane that inundated east Texas, Louisiana and Arkansas.

The violence of this storm on Lake Erie caused major damage and flooding especially at Erie, Pennsylvania and Buffalo as waves rolled the length of the lake. Many vessels were in distress, and five sank on Lake Erie the evening of October 14th. The schooner *George M. Case* foundered off Port Colborne, Ontario. Four men were rescued off her spars. The schooner *O.M. Bond* was driven ashore west of Rondeau Point where the men climbed the rigging, but two were drowned when the mainmast fell. Ashtabula, Ohio was the scene of another disaster as the schooner *Nevada* was beached. Fortunately for her crew, Captain John Duff of the schooner *C.B. Benson* was able to send a boat to their rescue. The scow *W.R. Hanna*, loading stone at Kelleys Island, was sunk in North Bay.

Reports of much wreckage above Erie and off Long Point initiated searches by several vessels. Some five days after the storm, a telegram was received from A.F. Barker, one of the *Mitchell's* owners, inquiring about her fate. For several days the only missing boat on the lake was the *Belle*. The newspapers reported that a brother of Captain Truman G. Rusho, William Rusho, of Clayton, New York, had traveled to Erie to check out wreckage that included a door frame and door whose brass sill had printed in brass tacks the word Belle. William Rusho also identified a scuttlebutt (cask of fresh water) and yawl fragment as belonging to the ill-fated schooner. In addition to his brother, William lost his sister Mrs. Phebe Dick, the cook, her husband and another brother-in-law. All told, there were eight crew aboard the *Mitchell*, at least five of whom were from Clayton.

Are these barrels scuttlebutts, or were they used to lift the masts after the *Belle Mitchell* sank?

About two weeks after the storm a letter was received from Captain John Carr of the schooner *Hartford* reporting he saw the *Belle* in distress. It was also Captain Carr who later found spars broken off, but attached to a wreck off Long Point cut, near where the *Hartford* and *Mitchell* had parted company in the hurricane.

An old sailor named Seymore, from Grindstone Island, remembered the *Belle* was difficult to sail but Captain Truman Rusho took pride in his ability to manage the ship and liked to carry lots of sail. According to a vessel agent, as he began his last voyage, Captain Rusho gave an eerie prediction. He said, "We have been having such long spells of fine weather for this time of the year that I expect to see something to make up for it." Unfortunately for the crew of the schooner *Belle Mitchell,* the captain's assessment of the fall weather was all too correct.

The Wreck Today

The wreck of the *Belle Mitchell* sits on a sand bottom and has not been disturbed by man since the day she went down. Beginning at the bow, the bowsprit is broken and one anchor remains on the port side. There is a windlass, mainmast hole, winch, pump, and the first of three hatches. A capstan follows with another small hatch revealing an offset centerboard. The mainmast hole is octagonal and surrounded by a fife rail. Behind this is a second pump, another sheet winch, a hold, and opening for the cabin.

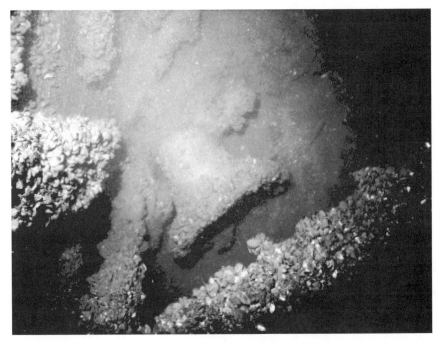

Bell of the *Belle Mitchell*

In the cabin area are two stoves, dishes, and the compass base. The wheel is aft of this. The cabin top lies off the port side of the stern. Following the chain that snakes along the port gunnels, you will find two large barrels on the outside, but leaning upright against the schooner. A brass bell that has the words "bell foundry" lies in the bow to the port side near the windlass. The foremast is off the port bow and perpendicular to the boat.

For now, this "Belle" of a schooner will remain a secret in order to keep her time capsule of artifacts intact.

Capstan

Dish in the cabin area

Stove in the cabin area and wheel at the stern
All images by the authors.

The *Belle Mitchell* on the bottom. Painting by Georgann Wachter

OGDENSBURG

Official #:	none	**Site #:**	22

Location: 7.8 miles at 175° T off the entrance to Mentor Harbor, Ohio

Coordinates: GPS: 41 50.418 81 21.964   LORAN: 43987.0 57743.5

Lies:	bow west	**Depth:**	65 feet
Type:	wood propeller	**Cargo:**	wheat, flour, passengers

Power: vertical, direct-acting steam

Owner(s) Northern Transportation Company

Built: 1852 by Moses and Quayle at Ohio City (Cleveland), Ohio

Dimensions:	138' x 25' x 11'	**Tonnage:**	352

Date of Loss: Friday, September 30, 1864

Cause of Loss: collision

Ogdensburg

Authors' Collection

A Tragic History:

The *Ogdensburg* was first enrolled in May of 1852. She had an octagonal pilot house, white hull trimmed in green and a long cabin to accommodate passengers. A single mast behind her pilot house would sometimes be rigged for sailing. This augmented her vertical direct-acting steam engine. This canal sized steamer was only half way through her first season when she was involved in one of the greatest disasters in the history of the inland seas.

It was August 19, 1852 when the sidewheel steamer *Atlantic* set out from Buffalo with 500 to 600 passengers, most of whom were Norwegian immigrants. Shortly after midnight, as they approached Long Point, the watchman on the *Ogdensburg* noticed the *Atlantic* approaching. She was about three miles away. The crew of the *Atlantic* apparently mistook the propeller for a slower paced schooner. After the two vessels collided, both kept on course, but the *Atlantic* soon headed to the north shore as water poured into her bilges. Hearing shouts from the stricken passengers, Captain Richardson turned the *Ogdensburg* back and rescued approximately 250 people. Captain Petty of the *Atlantic* was injured and unable to restore calm to the panicking Norwegian immigrants There were charges of bad blood, inadequate lights, and incompetence between the vessels. Approximately 250 people were lost, making this the fifth worst loss of life disaster on the Great Lakes.

Story of the Loss:

The *Ogdensburg* continued to run as a passenger and freight boat, connecting the Ogdensburg Railroad

Oiler from the *Ogdensburg* was removed by divers in the 1970s.

with points as far west as Chicago. On September 30 of 1864, the *Ogdensburg* left Cleveland under command of Captain Tyler. She carried a load of wheat for her home port of Ogdensburg, New York. Seeing the lights of another vessel closer to shore, the captain changed course to allow more sea room.

COLLISION BETWEEN THE STEAMER ATLANTIC AND PROPELLER OGDENSBURG ON LAKE ERIE, N. Y.

Collision of the steamer *Atlantic* and the *Ogdensburg*

Unfortunately, the other vessel did likewise, and the *Ogdensburg* came into collision with the schooner *Snowbird* of Oswego, New York. The schooner, running before a strong northeast breeze, continued on, as the crew of the *Ogdensburg* lowered her boats. Captain Tyler was the last to leave the boat, and he left barely in time. As the second lifeboat floated away, the steamer sank.

The Wreck Today:

This little steamer has a single boiler and fine old engine but, she sits down in the silt, making her a hard target to find. For many years she was known as the *"Mud Wreck"*. Early divers removed her anchors and one of these anchors rests in front of Pickle Bills Restaurant in Grand River, Ohio.

Metal caps on pipes, with chain leading out of them, grace her deck. There is a fine windlass at the bow. With the exception of occasional uprights, the sides of the vessel have disappeared into the silt. Aft of the bow section,

Foredeck hatch

there is a centerboard. Swimming on toward the stern, the best part of the wreck is yet to come. Her antique boiler and cute, yes cute, little engine rises up from the silty bottom. A steam pipe still connects the single boiler to the vertical direct-acting engine. Aft of the machinery are fishnet covered posts that outline the shape of the transom.

Taken as our vessel headed east, this side scan image shows the intact bow pointing west, and her machinery at the top of the scan.

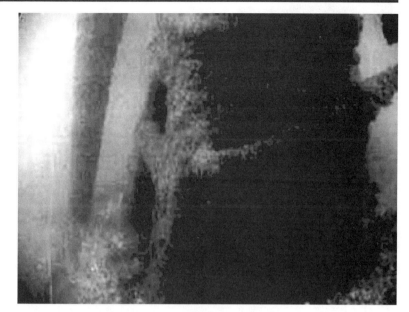

Video captures by Mike Wachter.

Engine

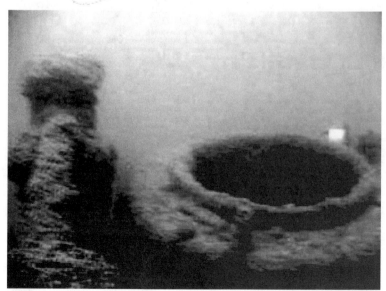

Ogdensburg
138′ x 25′ x 11′
By Georgann Wachter
not to scale

Boiler

PATAPSCO

Official #: 54617   **Site #:** 29

Location: west side of Presque Isle, 5.8 miles at 50° T from Walnut Creek, Pennsylvania entrance

Coordinates: GPS: 42 07.883 80 09.096   LORAN: 44348.0 58450.0

Lies: east / west   **Depth:** 25 feet

Type: dredge   **Cargo:** none

Power: towed

Owner(s) Arundel & Monkers Construction Company of Baltimore, Maryland

Built: 1901 at Port Richmond, New York

Dimensions: 80' x 28' x 7.1'   **Tonnage:** 2304 gross   292 net

Date of Loss: Friday, June 27, 1930

Cause of Loss: sprung a leak

Dredge Barge similar to Patapsco

Great Lakes Historical Society, Bowen Collection

Story of the Loss:

The *Patapsco* was built for the B&O Railroad Company, and her first home port was Baltimore, Maryland. In the early 1930s, the Sommerheim Water Intake was built west of the Presque Isle Peninsula to supply water for the city of Erie, Pennsylvania. The *Patapsco* was working on this project when she went to the bottom. The March 1931, *Marine Review* reported that a boiler and some of her mechanicals were salvaged shortly after her loss.

The Wreck Today:

As you look south from the lake, you can count a series of break walls. The *Patapsco* is located about one half mile from shore between the ninth and tenth pile of rocks off of beach #2.

Erie Water Works sits inside the bay at Presque Isle. The *Patapsco* was lost building a new water intake for the City of Erie.

Although predominantly sand, this area has a mud drop off pocked with crayfish holes, running parallel to the shore. Local divers call the drop off the "honey hole" because it collects debris and trees. The wreck lies perpendicular to the shore in the bottom of the drop off. The area is heavily scoured by sand, producing unusual and interesting formations on the lake bottom.

The body of the wreck lies east of the beach 2 intake. She has huge rough hewn wood beams. A boom about 30 feet long and some three feet high, an "A"-frame and other machinery provide points of interest for the diver. There are also a couple of 72" capped iron pipes that were either a part of the dredge plant or used to float intake pipes out to the site.

Side scan image of the *Patapsco*.

THEODORE PERRY

Official #:   24163   **Site #:**   23

Location: 33.1 miles at 351° T off Fairport Harbor entrance, 27.1 miles at 92° T off Erieau, Ontario

Coordinates: GPS: 42 14.450   81 22.685   LORAN: 44157.5   57829.1

Lies: bow west   **Depth:**   80 feet

Type: schooner with three masts   **Cargo:**   coal

Power: towed

Owner(s)   James H. Prentice of Saginaw, Michigan

Built: as a schooner in 1855 by Bidwell & Banta of Buffalo, New York

Dimensions: 137' x 26' x 11'   **Tonnage:**   261

Date of Loss: Friday, July 22, 1887

Cause of Loss: hull failure in storm

The Theodore Perry was under tow as demonstrated in this
photo of a steamer with consorts in tow.

Great Lakes Historical Society, Bowen Collection

Story of the Loss:

As the age of steam power had dawned, the once proud schooner *Theodore Perry* was now relegated to the status of a barge. Working as a consort with others of her kind, she would be tethered to a line and hauled to her destination by a steam powered vessel. This is how she left Buffalo on the day of her loss. The *Perry*, and other consorts were headed for Saginaw, Michigan in tow of the steamer *D.W. Powers*. The barge was one in a string of vessels in a tow that included the schooners *B.B. Buckout, Wyadotte,* and *Senator Blood*. About 9 pm, a stiff northerly wind caused the seas to grow. Two hours later, the *Theodore Perry's* tow line parted. Captain McCormick checked the bilges and found no water. However, he noticed that the seams were parting on the starboard side and immediately called all of his crew on deck.

The crew and one passenger, Neil McLane, scrambled to the deck and attempted to lower the yawl. Waves were now crashing over the vessel. Water coming in through the split seams in the starboard side caused her to settle lower in the water. One wave washed the cabin off, taking the cook, Mary Wisminter, with it. Captain McCormick climbed onto the cabin roof as the *Perry* settled. Mate Hugh Deering got onto the forecastle deck. The seas continued to toss them back and forth as they yelled to one another to keep up hope as the night wore on.

Deering was unconscious when, 11 hours after the vessel had gone to the bottom, Captain McCormick finally attracted the attention of the propeller *Alaska*. After his rescue, the captain chartered a yacht to search for his lost men. Among the lost was Charles Copley, son-in-law of the owner, J.H. Prentice.

The Wreck Today:

The coal cargo, location, size, and barge configuration lead us to believe that this wreck location is the *Theodore Perry*. Beginning at the bow, there is an anchor on the starboard side, a windlass, toppled pump, and broken stump of a mast. Further aft, another mast lies to port next to a second set of deadeyes. A second pump is on the port stern near a small hatch, and her wheel stands tall, still in place.

There is a large hole in the port side, which appears to have been caused by her anchor, unless the newspapers were wrong and it was the port hull that gave way.

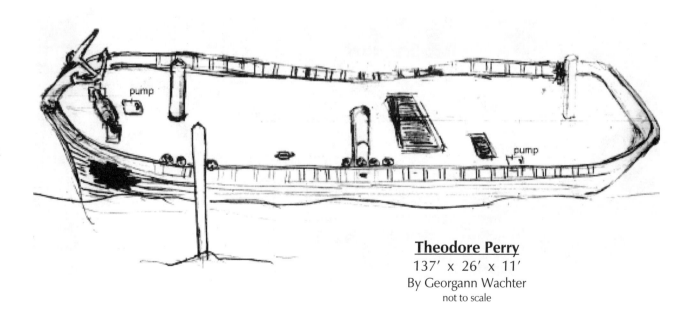

Theodore Perry
137' x 26' x 11'
By Georgann Wachter
not to scale

C.H. Plummer

Official #:	126494	**Site #:**	7
Location:	off Carpenters Point, Kelleys Island to the west of the Newman Dock		
Coordinates:	GPS: 41 35.859 82 43.914		
Lies:	bow northeast	**Depth:**	18 feet
Type:	scow	**Cargo:**	stone
Power:	sail		
Owner(s)	A.J. Helbing, Sandusky Coal Company		
Built:	1888 by John Monk at Sandusky, Ohio		
Dimensions:	116.5' x 28.3' x 8.2'	**Tonnage:**	219
Date of Loss:	Wednesday, November 21, 1888		
Cause of Loss:	fire		

Kelleys Stone Dock
with the *H.G. Cleveland*

Authors' Collection

Story of the Loss:

The barge *C.H. Plummer* was built over the winter of 1887 and 1888, and launched in Sandusky on June 16, 1888. She was built for use in the coal and stone trade. Her first voyage took her to East Saginaw, Michigan with a load of stone.

At the close of her first season, disaster by fire overtook the barge *Plummer*. She had been on a stone run from Kelleys Island to Cleveland. The crew was on shore at Kelleys when the fire started in the cabin at about 11 in the evening. A bucket brigade was quickly formed in an effort to minimize the extent of the fire. However, her cabin, most of her deck, and her stern were badly damaged. She sank (or was scuttled) with her sixty-five yards of stone a couple of hours after the fire started. One newspaper suggested that, when she sank, she severed the underwater power cable between Sandusky and Kelleys Island, Ohio.

South of Carpenters Point and west of the Cameron Road Newman Ferry Dock at Kelleys, lays the remains of a scow. Historian Frank Hamilton indicated that this was the location of the wreck of the *C.H. Plummer*. As it was in front of his home on Kelleys Island, his information should be accurate. Another possibility is that this site is the burned hull of the tug *Relief*, which was towed to the west end of Kelleys Island and scuttled in July of 1884.

The Wreck Today:

This site has a mud and rock bottom topography that gets weedy in the late summer. The sides of the vessel are flattened and the bow has been pulled off. Because there is no cargo evident, we can not be certain this is the *Plummer* and not the *Relief*. Since the *Plummer* sank at the dock, it is concievable that her stone cargo was salvaged.

Divers should watch for heavy boat traffic in the area and the semi-submerged old docks nearby.

The Kelleys Island area gets a lot of ferry traffic. Pictured here is the *Kayla Marie*.

RED BIRD

Official #: C72960   **Site #:** 25

Location: 11.8 miles at 67° T off Fairport Harbor entrance, 15.3 miles at 348° T off Ashtabula

Coordinates: GPS: 41 50.120 81 04.177   LORAN: 44035.6 57898.1

Lies: east / west   **Depth:** 25 feet

Type: two masted scow schooner   **Cargo:** telephone poles

Power: sail

Owner(s) H. Minnes of Welland, Ontario

Built: 1870 at Hamilton, Ontario by R. McPherson

Dimensions: 64.6' x 17.8' x 4.4'   **Tonnage:** 39

Date of Loss: before 1903

Cause of Loss: unknown

Scow Schooner similar to the Red Bird

Authors' collection

Story of the Loss:

There have been may vessels that carried the name *Red Bird*. T. Wiard had a 50 ton scow named *Red Bird* built by Joel Norton and a man named Platts near this location circa 1852. However, despite being constructed near the wreck site, it is purportedly not the shipwreck at this location. The wrecked *Red Bird* is apparently the Canadian scow listed above. The wreck gave its name to Madison, Ohio's, Red Bird Road. The road's name is listed in a 1908 atlas as Platt's Road (named for the vessel's builder). Local lore reported by Madison historian, Luanna Billington, is that "people would take the path in carriages to see the schooner." The site became such a popular place to picnic, or to wile away a leisurely afternoon, that the path that was worn by people on foot, horseback, and carriages turned into a full blown road. Platts Road was officially renamed Red Bird Road (named for the shipwreck) on May 6, 1952. Although we do not know the exact date of the sinking, the local lore and the road name appearing on platt maps suggest the *Red Bird* sank between 1900 and 1903. The wreck first appears on a 1903 chart.

Divers located this wreck about 5/8 of a mile north northwest of the foot of Red Bird Road many years ago. A female statue overlooking the lake is still a favorite landmark.

The Wreck Today:

A rock bottom at a depth of 15 feet abruptly gives way to an east / west trench that is approximately 25 feet deep and 250 feet long. The bottom of the trench is mud and numerous trees have been deposited inside its walls. Among the debris trapped in the trench is planking, ballast stone, and spars from the *Red Bird*.

Our dive time in this area was limited and we were pleased to find the ship remains in the trench. However, we are certain that a more thorough search of this area would turn up additional parts of the scow schooner *Red Bird*.

Red Bird beach in Madison, Ohio as it appeared on an August 16, 1910 postcard.
Photo from the personal collection of Carl Thomas Engel

ROB ROY

Official #: C94925   **Site #:** 31

Location: 2.4 miles at 32° T off Erie, Pennsylvania's Harbor entrance

Coordinates: GPS: 42 11.095   80 02.639   LORAN: 44392.6   58517.4

Lies: bow west   **Depth:** 40 feet

Type: schooner barge   **Cargo:** 800 tons of coal

Power: towed

Owner(s) Canadian Navigation Company of Toronto, Ontario

Built: 1897 by A. Hepburn at Picton, Ontario

Dimensions: 144' x 31' x 10'   **Tonnage:** 470

Date of Loss: Sunday, September 17, 1916

Cause of Loss: sprung a leak

Rob Roy

Private collection of Ralph Roberts

Story of the Loss:

In tow of the tug *Home Rule,* the Canadian schooner barge *Rob Roy* cleared Erie on Sunday, September 17, 1916 with a load of coal for Port Colborne, Ontario. When only three miles out, she encountered such heavy seas that Master Alfred Dane ordered the crew to the pumps. Unfortunately, the siphon was clogged so attempts to rid the hold of water were for naught. The tow attempted to turn about to Erie. But, the water gained very rapidly forcing the *Home Rule* to cut the *Rob Roy* loose. The tug then took off the barge's sailors and sloshed on to Dunkirk, New York. At Dunkirk, ten inches of water was removed from the tug's hold. The *Rob Roy's* hull had been in poor condition for some time.

The schooner barge was named for the Scottish Robin Hood, Red Robert MacGregor. In an attempt to regain his homestead and cattle, MacGregor (aka Rob Roy) made war on the Duke of Montrose in 1716. He and his clan succeeded in this endeavor after kidnapping the Duke and seizing all the cattle in the district.

The Wreck Today:

Much of the midsection and stern of the *Rob Roy* lies buried in the mud. The windlass is on the port bow with chain leading off in two directions. The ineffective siphon pump lies forward of the this, and a ladder is against the windlass. There are large piles of her coal cargo. Off the stern is some machinery that looks to be her steering gear.

This wreck managed to stay hidden from searchers just off the track into Erie for 90 years. Figures it was named for the Robin Hood of Scotland.

Taken as our boat ran northeast, this side scan image of the *Rob Roy* shows the stern silted over and the bow pointing to the west.

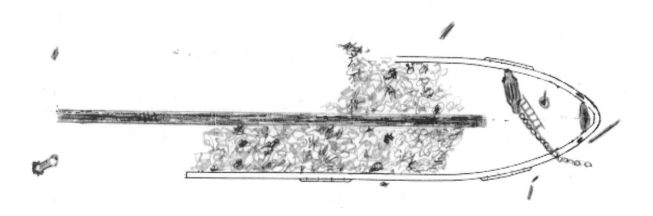

Drawing of the *Rob Roy* as she sits today. By Georgann Wachter.

W.R. Stafford

Official #:	81126		**Site #:**	8
Location:	Shoreline Park, Sandusky, Ohio			
Coordinates:	GPS: 41 27.652 82 42.480			
Lies:	bow west	**Depth:**	8 feet	
Type:	wood sandsucker	**Cargo:**	none	
Power:	500 horse power steam engine			
Owner(s)	Kelleys Island Lime and Transportation Company of Sandusky, Ohio			
Built:	1886 by F.W. Wheeler & Company at West Bay City, Michigan			
Dimensions:	195' x 34' x 13.3'	**Tonnage:**	686 gross 398 net	
Date of Loss:	1930			
Cause of Loss:	abandoned, leaked, burned			

W.R. Stafford

Great Lakes Historical Society

Story of the Loss:

The oak steamer *W.R. Stafford* was originally built as a bulk freighter. She was used in the lumber trade by her namesake, William Rogers Stafford, who owned large tracks of timber in the state of Michigan.

In 1913, the vessel was converted to sandsucker at Sandusky, Ohio. She ended her useful life in 1925, and was abandoned for age in Sandusky Bay's western slip of the B&O Railroad Dock. Sitting at the dock for several years, she finally rotted and sank in place. Some time in 1930, a fire burned her to the water-line.

The Wreck Today:

The rudder, other artifacts and information on the *Stafford* are displayed at the Sandusky Maritime Museum. The wreck is located at Shoreline Park between Franklin and Warren Streets.

Viewable from the shore, the ribs and keel of this shipwreck stick up from the mud bottom. Because of her easy access from shore, she was considered a candidate for training students in the art of underwater archaeology by the Maritime Archaeological Survey Team. This stagnant, shallow water site gets lots of fertilizer runoff and sunshine. As a result, the water here is usually weedy and uninviting. We suggest you stay dry and view this one from the park. That's what we did!

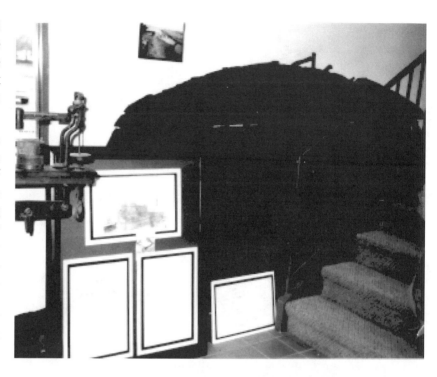

Stafford display at the Sandusky Maritime Museum

The *W.R. Stafford* is best viewed from the side of the old B&O Pier at Shoreline Park. Look closely along the edge and you can see remains, especially when the water is clear in the spring of the year. The Sandusky Yacht Club is in the background.

Sugar Barge

Official #:   C ?   **Site #:**   14

Location: one quarter mile east of Vermilion, Ohio Harbor entrance

Coordinates: GPS: PA: 41 25.755   82 21.182

Lies: unknown   **Depth:**   8 feet

Type: wood barge   **Cargo:**   sugar or liquor

Power: towed

Owner(s)   unknown

Built: unknown

Dimensions: see photo for estimate   **Tonnage:**   unknown

Date of Loss: Summer 1924 ?

Cause of Loss: storm

Sugar Barge aground at Vermilion

Great Lakes Historical Society

Story of the Loss:

According to Vermilion historian George Wakefield, a Canadian tug with two sugar barges in tow got caught in a northeast storm on a summer day in about 1924. The first one broke up, and the other one came ashore at the Linwood Park resort area. This sixty-two acre resort was established in 1884. Its cottages still exist today and offer a Victorian feel as you enter the gates. In the past there was a hotel, bathhouse, carnival games, and a steam driven carousel.

In searching for a more exact date for the loss of the barge, two significant hints to solve the mystery emerged. In *Through These Gates* (Linwood Park) by Karen and Ray Boas, it was intimated that perhaps these "sugar" barges were not reported because they were actually rum runners. It seems a fully loaded barge went aground and was raided by the local townspeople. The captain dared not report the theft of his illegal cargo.

Another possibility for the loss of the barge was the wild weather that accompanied the Sandusky/Lorain tornado of June 28, 1924. This tornado is still the deadliest in Ohio history. Twenty-five businesses were lost in Sandusky before the wind headed out over the lake. In Huron, which is about 10 miles east-southeast of Sandusky, violent winds were reported, and there was significant damage. That storm went

The City of Lorain digs out after the 1924 tornado.
Photo from Lorain Public Library

northeastward through the town and out over the lake to join the greater storm moving eastward from Sandusky. Nearer Vermilion, the storm destroyed the Lorain Municipal Bathhouse. Traveling inland, the tornado leveled 500 homes and killed fifteen people who were in the State Theater. All told, there were seventy-two people killed that day in Lorain, a city of thirty-seven thousand.

The *Sugar Barge* lies to the east of the Vermilion River, off Linwood Park.

The Wreck Today:

This wreck is located off the last set of groins to the east of the river. It is about fifty feet north of the markers that are set for swimmers off Linwood Park. We dinged a propeller while sidescanning the area and a friend almost hit the remains with his Sea Doo. As a result, we have not yet been on the wreck, and we advise others to exercise great caution. This one might best be done on a dingy or from shore.

VERMILION SMALL BARGE

Official #: unknown   **Site #:** 13

Location: 9.0 miles at 000° T from west end of the breakwater at the entrance to Vermilion River

Coordinates: GPS: 41 33.518   82 21.924

Lies: bow southwest   **Depth:** 48 feet

Type: wood barge   **Cargo:** unknown

Power: towed

Owner(s) unknown

Built: unknown

Dimensions: 40' x 13' x 4'   **Tonnage:** approximately 17 gross

Date of Loss: unknown

Cause of Loss: unknown

Typical Wooden Pile Driver Barge

Great Lakes Historical Society

Story of the Loss:

We must admit that we found this site while looking for the *Anthony Wayne*, a sidewheel steamer that exploded off of Vermilion, Ohio. This, once again, proves that, often the shipwreck found by wreck hunters is not the one for which the searcher is looking.

It will take more research to narrow this one down. However, there is a possibility that the *Vermilion Small Barge* is the scow schooner *Lilly* that capsized off of Vermilion in 1862. Our one attempt to measure the craft indicated that this vessel is shorter than the *Lilly*, though the breadth and depth are dead on. Given the limited visibility on the occasions when we have tried to work this site, there is a chance that our length measurement is off a bit.

The *Lilly* was built in 1858 by Mathew Barringer in Sandusky, Ohio. She measured 58' by 13'4" by 4'2". The *Lilly's* captain went down with his ship when it foundered 10 miles off of Vermilion. One young boy and another crewman were rescued from the *Lilly's* boat eighteen hours after the *Lilly* went to the bottom.

Another possibility is that this small vessel was a pile driver or net stake puller.

The Wreck Today:

This small barge is located on a sand bottom. The bow and stern are tapered. Some planks are missing from the deck, revealing horizontal knees. At each end is a five inch diameter iron ring. The bow has what appears to be a nine inch diameter mast hole. The construction of the *Little Barge* strikes us as very old. There is some debris off of her western end that we have yet to explore.

This will be a hard target to find because of its small size. She sits in an area not noted for good visibility

Line drawing of a wooden stake barge. This vessel would be used to drive stakes for fish nets and then pull those same stakes at season's end

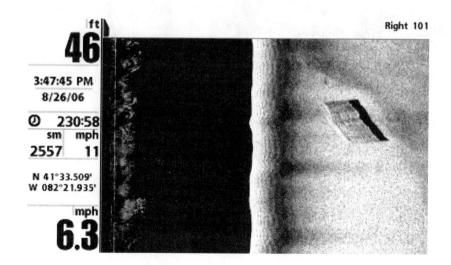

Side scan image of the *Vermilion Small Barge*. Side scan by the authors.

GEORGE J. WHELAN

Official #:	207617	**Site #:**	33
Location:	9.6 miles at 306° T from entrance to Barcelona Harbor, New York		
Coordinates:	GPS: 42 25.555 79 44.986		
Lies:	bow north	**Depth:**	145 to 165 feet
Type:	sandsucker	**Cargo:**	limestone
Power:	800 hourse power steam engine		
Owner(s)	Kelleys Island Lime and Transportation Company of Sandusky, Ohio		
Built:	1910 by Toledo Shipbuilding Company at Toledo, Ohio		
Dimensions:	237' x 40' x 17'	**Tonnage:**	1293 gross
Date of Loss:	Tuesday, July 29, 1930		
Cause of Loss:	cargo shifted in a storm		

George J. Whelan as the Claremont

Great Lakes Historical Society

Story of the Loss:

The *Whelan* was built as the bulk freighter *Erwin L. Fisher*. Sold to Canadian interests, she collided with another steamer and sank in the Detroit River in 1912. This incident killed three men. As the French owned *Port de Caen*, she was used to transport coal across the English Channel during World War I. In 1915 she was sunk by a mine in the English Channel. Raised and rebuilt by Canadian owners, there were two more name changes, *Bayersher* in 1922 and *Claremont* in 1923, before she was converted to a crane equipped sandsucker in her final year.

First mate Robert A. Endelman of the steamer *Amasa Stone* had the night watch and was guiding his vessel west toward Erie, Pennsylvania to pick up a coal cargo. Feeling his way through the darkness of the night, he was startled when suddenly he heard a cry. By the second call, he knew that "men were floating around in the water helpless" (*Buffalo Evening News*). Endelman ordered the engines stopped and sent the wheelsman to awaken Captain Walter McNeill. With no engine noise, voices became clear. "Help! Lower a boat." Soon, all of the *Stone's* crew was awake and, despite there being a heavy sea on, there was no lack of volunteers to help fellow seamen. Captain McNeil was quoted as saying, "Unless you have sailed the lakes, you don't know what it means to locate six men swimming around in the night time (*Buffalo Evening News*)."

By 3:35 am Captain McNeill had wired the Coast Guard that the *George J. Whelan* had gone to the bottom. Battling a heavy southwest wind, rescuers headed to the area where the *Stone* was searching. Tragically, the only survivors were the six men found in the first three hours by Captain McNeill's crew.

The *Whelan* had left Sandusky on Sunday afternoon. It was her maiden voyage under ownership of the Kelleys Island Lime and Transportation Company. A foreshadowing of the unlucky trip came at a stop in Cleveland, Ohio. That evening, watchman Frank Looker was crushed by a loading bucket. Looker's brother-in-law, Jess Paliderer, left the vessel to tend to transportation of Looker's body. Continuing on to Buffalo, New York, the *Whelan* encountered a severe thunderstorm that sent water into the holds. This

The lost captain and surviving crew of the *George Whelan*. *Buffalo Evening News*

caused the limestone cargo to shift to port. Several of the crew were sent below with shovels to try to redistribute the load in an attempt to right the ship. It's thought that the fifteen crew members that did not survive were trapped below decks, probably in the cargo holds. However, wheelsman Eckart Lang said that Captain Tom Waage called the crew on deck before the ship suddenly rolled over. Six "lucky" men sat on her overturned hull for about a half hour before it sank from under them. Having no life jacket, Lang began to swim to shore. Fortunately for him, the *Amasa Stone* found the *Whelan's* crew. Captain Waage and eleven others did not survive.

The Wreck Today:

Today the *Whelan* lays on her port side ¾ turtled. Though the bottom is about 140 feet, divers penetrating the wreck (not recommended without proper training and equipment), have reported depths of up to 165 feet.

The mooring line is usually tied to the rudder skeg, which makes a great photo opportunity, as her four-bladed propeller and rudder are in the background. Just off the stern, the bow of a lifeboat rises out of the silt. There is a block and tackle nearby. Burbot often rest in the *Whelan's* portholes. Several of the portholes are open, a fact that may have hastened the demise of the ship in the sudden summer storm. A glance inside reveals the contents of each room and the wood paneled walls of her cabins. At the stern is a stairwell and corridor. Moving forward, there is much debris under the vessel, and it is very apparent that this is a near virgin shipwreck. At the bow there are winches and an anchor.

Part of the allure of this dive is the extensive debris field that lays to the west of the hull. The debris field holds air vents, lights, and other items that came loose as the *Whelan* went down.

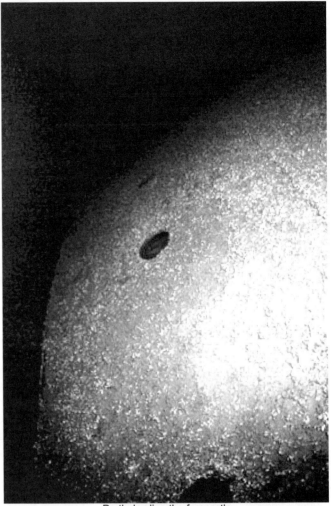

Portholes line the forecastle

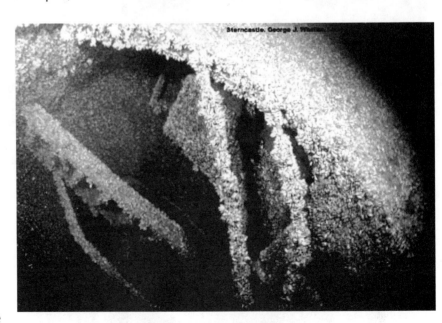

Ladder and companionway at stern

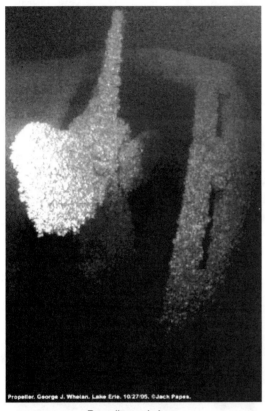

Propeller and skeg.

Lifeboat

Underwater photos by Jack Papes

Amidships

Wisconsin

Official #:	none	**Site #:**	2
Location:	2.2 miles at 114° T from West Sister Island Light		
Coordinates:	GPS: 41 43.246 83 04.381 LORAN: 43679.1 56824.3		
Lies:	bow east	**Depth:**	35 feet
Type:	sidewheel steamer	**Cargo:**	none
Power:	crosshead engine, 26' diameter sidewheels with two boilers and 60" cylinders.		
Owner(s)	George Davis of Buffalo, New York and Captain T.J. Titus		
Built:	1838 by G.W. Jones at Conneaut, Ohio		
Dimensions:	218.8' x 30' x 14'	**Tonnage:**	887
Date of Loss:	Wednesday, August 24, 1853		
Cause of Loss:	collision		

Wisconsin

Louden Wilson Drawing

Story of the Loss:

Launched in November of 1837, the *Wisconsin* was completed in 1838. Captain G.F. Power was her commander at the time. Originally she was 157 feet long with a 29 foot beam. She had a dining cabin with sixty berths for gentlemen, ten staterooms for families, and fifty ladies berths. In 1844 she was lengthened sixty feet and her hold was deepened three and one half feet. Her usual run was to Buffalo, Detroit, Milwaukee, and Chicago. In 1847 she collided with the steamer *Nile* of off Milwaukee, Wisconsin.

This vessel had one of the oldest engines of any ship sunk in the Great Lakes. Her power plant had been in two Hudson River steamers, the *Constitution* and the *Ohio*, before 1838. This machinery was constructed by J. Birbeck in New York City.

While running on the Buffalo Stock line, the *Wisconsin* had left Toledo, Ohio and was on her way to Sandusky. The night was clear and Captain Hayes had seen the upbound propeller *Brunswick*. As the two vessels approached it appeared they would collide. The alarmed captain ordered the *Wisconsin* stopped. Perhaps through a misinterpretation of an order by the helmsman, the two vessels came together, with the *Brunswick* smashing the sidewheeler's bow so thoroughly that the *Wisconsin* sunk in five to ten minutes. Opportunely, the crew was rescued by the *Brunswick*.

Some four years later, diver Mr. Quigley of sidewheel steamer *Atlantic's* salvage fame removed two anchors, chain, and some machinery from the derelict. At that time, she was described as listing to port with most of her bulwarks, main deck, and arches gone.

The Wreck Today:

The remains of the *Wisconsin* rise about nine feet off the mud bottom. Regrettably, the two opportunities we have had to explore this wreck have offered only two

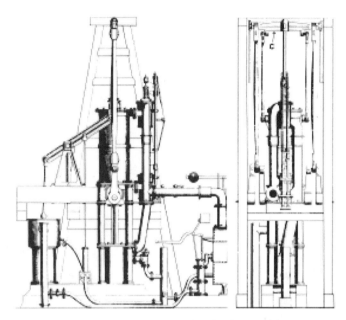

The *Wisconsin's* crosshead engine is one of the oldest in the Great Lakes.

to four feet of visibility. The boilers and pipes are present along with other machinery. Wood elements of the wreck stretch across a fairly large area but the limited visibility makes it difficult to tell what is what on the bottom. There is a cylindrical hole that will admit a diver. We anticipate that further exploration will reveal more of the interesting design of this vessel and her early power plant.

The *Wisconsin* sank quickly after being struck by the *Brunswick*.

BIBLIOGRAPHY

BOOKS

Barrett, Harry B. <u>Lore and Ledgends of Long Point</u>. Paterson Creek Press, 2000

Barry, James P. <u>Wrecks and Rescues of the Great Lakes, A Photographic History</u>. La Jolla, California: Howell and North Books, 1981

<u>Beesons Marine Directory of the Northwest Lakes (various years)</u>. Chicago, Illinois: Harvey C. Beeson.

Berger, Todd R. and Dempster, Daniel E. <u>Lighthouses of the Great Lakes</u>. Stillwater, MN: Voyager Press, 2004

Bowen, Dana T. <u>Shipwrecks of the Lakes</u>. Cleveland, Ohio: Freshwater Press, 1952.

Brown, George <u>The Fisheries and Fishing Industry of the U.S.</u> Good and Associates Washington Government Printing Office, 1887

Doner, Mary Francis. <u>The Salvager</u>. Minneapolis, Minnesota: Ross and Haines, Inc., 1958

Francis, David W. and Diane <u>Cedar Point: The Queen of American Watering Places</u>, Fairview Park, Ohio, 1995.

<u>Great Lakes Red Book (various years)</u>. Saint Clair Shores, Michigan: The Fourth Seacoast Publishing Company.

Greenwood, John O. <u>Namesakes 1930 - 1955</u>. Cleveland, Ohio: Freshwater Press, Inc., 1995.

Greenwood, John O. <u>Namesakes 1920 - 1929</u>. Cleveland, Ohio: Freshwater Press, Inc., 1984.

Greenwood, John O. <u>Namesakes 1910 - 1919</u>. Cleveland, Ohio: Freshwater Press, Inc., 1986.

Greenwood, John O. <u>Namesakes 1900 - 1909</u>. Cleveland, Ohio: Freshwater Press, Inc., 1987.

Greenwood, John O. <u>Greenwood's Guide to Great Lakes Shipping (various years)</u>. Cleveland, Ohio: Freshwater Press, Inc.

Herdendorf, Charles E. and Pansing, Linda L <u>Shipwrecks of the Lake Erie Islands Region Part I Kelleys Island</u>. Vermilion, OH, Great Lakes Historical Society Peachman Lake Erie Research Center, 2005

Heyl, Eric. <u>Early American Steamers, Vols I - VI</u>. Buffalo, New York: published by the author at 136 West Oakwood Place, 1961 - 1969.

<u>History of Lorain Lighthouse</u>, Lorain, Ohio; The Black River Historical Society.

Kendrick, Isabelle <u>Al & Isabelle Kendrick Lighthouse Keepers</u>. Port Colborne Ontario: Self Published

<u>Lakelore</u>. Simcoe, Ontario: circa 1974.

Liebenthal, Dale E., J.A. Fuller, and Constance J. Livchak <u>Archeological Search for Shipwrecks in the Vicinity of Kelleys Island</u>. Columbus, OH: Ohio Division of Geological Survey, 2006

Lytle, William. <u>Merchant Steam Vessels of the U.S. 1807 - 1868</u>. Mystic, Connecticut: Steamship Historical Society of America, 1952.

MacDonald, Robert J. and David Frew. <u>Home Port Erie</u>. Erie , Pennsylvania, Erie County Historical Society, 1997.

Mansfield, J.B., ed. <u>History of the Great Lakes</u>, Two volumes. Chicago: J.H. Beers and Company, 1899. Reprint edition, Cleveland: Freshwater Press, 1972

Meakin, Alexander C. <u>The Story of the Great Lakes Towing Company</u>. Vermilion, Ohio: The Great Lakes Historical Society, 1984.

<u>Merchant Vessels of the U.S. (various years)</u>. Washington: Government Printing Office.

Mills, John M. <u>Canadian Coastal and Inland Steam Vessels, 1809 – 1930</u>. Providence, Rhode Island: The Steamship Historical Society of America, Inc., 1979.

Prothero, Frank. <u>The Good Years</u>. Bellville, Ontario, Mika Publishing, 1973.

Prothero, Frank and Nancy. <u>Tales of the North Shore</u>. Port Stanley, Ontario: Nan-Sea Publications, 1987.

Prothero, Frank and Nancy. <u>Memories, A History of Port Burwell</u>. Port Stanley, Ontario: Nan-Sea Publications, 1986.

Sabic, Christopher R. <u>Phase I Archaeological Investigation of the Barcelona Shipwreck, Lake Erie, Chautauqua County, New York</u>. Vergennes, VT: Lake Champlain Maritime Museum, 2000

Shaefer, Mary Louise. <u>Mitchell Steamship Company 1800's to 1900's, A Great Lakes Saga</u>. Avon Lake, Ohio: self published.

Shanks, Ralph and York, Wick <u>The U.S. Lifesaving Service, Heroes, Rescues and Architecture of the Early Coast Guard</u>. Lisa Woo Shanks, Editor, 1996 reprinted 2000.

Stone, David. <u>Long Point, Last Port of Call</u>. Erin, Ontario: Boston Mills Press, 1988.

Swayze, David D. <u>Shipwreck!</u>. Boyne City, Michigan: Harbor House Publications, Inc., 1992.

U.S. Coast Guard, <u>Historically Famous Lighthouses</u> Washington: Public Information Division, United States Coast Guard, 1972

Wakefield , Ernest Henry <u>The Lighthouse That Wanted to Stay Lit</u>, Honors Press Inc., 1992.

Wendt, Gordon. <u>In the Wake of the Walk-in-the-Water</u>. Sandusky, Ohio: Commercial Printing Co., 1984

BIBLIOGRAPHY

PERIODICALS

Many articles from newspapers throughout the Great Lakes region were used to gather data for this book, particularly the *Plain Dealer* of Cleveland, Ohio and the *Sandusky Register*. Lighthouse articles include:

"The Lights and Lost Lights of Fairport Harbor", Timothy Harrison, Lighthouse Digest.

"Fouling the Nest in Lake Erie", E. Sharp, Detroit Free Press, July 10, 2003.

"West Sister Island National Wildlife Refuge", Lake Erie Charter Boat Association, 2003.

"Grim Walls of Lighthouse Are Memoirs of Service", Toledo Blade, February 15, 1929.

"The Lights of Cleveland," The Cleveland Leader, Sunday, November 25, 1900.

"Three Nights of Heroism," by Dennis L. Noble, Our Sister Service: The U.S. Life Saving Service, Fall, 1997.

"Samuel Butler: First Lighthouse Keeper in Fairport Harbor", The Lake County Historical Society Quarterly, Vol. 19, March, 1977.

Other articles are sited in the body of the text.

MISCELLANEOUS

A Brief History of Canadian Lighthouses: http://members.aol.com/stiffcrust/pharos/

Database of Walter Lewis: www.hhpl.on.ca/GreatLakes/

Database of David Swayze: www.greatlakeshistory.homestead.com/home.html

Lighthouse Digest Database: http://lhdigest.com/database/searchdatabase.cfm

Lighthouse Friends Database: http://www.lighthousefriends.com/

Lighthouses of the Great Lakes Database: http://lighthouse.boatnerd.com/gallery/Erie/default.htm

Lorian City History: http://www.loraincityhistory.org

U.S. Coast Guard Historic Lighthouses: www.uscg.mil/hq/gcp/history/WEBLIGHTHOUSES/LHOH.html

"Master Sheets", Historical Collections of the Great Lakes, Bowling Green State University, Bowling Green, Ohio.

Sandusky Library and *Sandusky Register* Historical Files, including:
"Frank Ritter and Cedar Point Lighthouse", Kurtz.
"Light Range Led Boats Into Bay", 10/7/1990.
"Lake Tonnage Sixty Years Ago", Star Journal.
"Thursday Service for Frank Ritter, Keeper of Light", 8/25/1953.
"The Lighthouse at Cedar Point has been ordered closed", 4/22/1904.

PHOTOGRAPHS & DRAWINGS

In addition to pictures from our private collection, photographs and drawings for this publication were provided by:

John Davis, Williamsville, New York

Harry Goodman, New Bern, North Carolina

Great Lakes Historical Society, Vermilion, Ohio.

Al Hart, Bay Village, Ohio.

Rutherford B. Hayes Presidential Center, Fremont, Ohio

Historical Collections of the Great Lakes, Bowling Green State University. Bowling Green, Ohio.

C. Patrick Labadie, Alpina, Michigan

Gerry Paine, Avon Lake, Ohio

Jack Papes, Akron, Ohio

Ralph Roberts, Saginaw, Michigan.

Jim Smith, Avon Lake, Ohio

Tom Wilson, New Market, Ontario

Georgann and Mike Wachter have been diving around the world since the mid 1970ies. Though sites in the Caribbean, Atlantic and Pacific have fascinated them, wreck research and diving the Great Lakes is their passion. This has resulted in four previous books, *Erie Wrecks, Erie Wrecks East, Erie Wrecks West* and *Erie Wrecks East, Second Edition*. In addition they have published articles in several magazines and newspapers, including: *Advanced Diver Magazine, Quantum* and *Inland Seas*. Their knowledge of the lakes has been cited in *Skin Diver, The Cleveland Plain Dealer, The Chicago Tribune* and *Cleveland Magazine*.

Mike and Georgann have held a variety of offices in dive clubs, including the Aqua Masters of Lakewood and Lake Erie Wreck Divers of Lorain, Ohio.

Both have been active in the Maritime Archaeological Survey Team (MAST) where Mike is past president and Georgann is current treasurer. Under Mike's tenure 6 shipwrecks in Ohio waters were moored for divers. They are members of the Great Lakes Historical Society, Vermilion, Ohio, Peachman Lake Erie Research Shipwreck Center (PLESRC), Technical Advisory Committee (TAC) and have been assistant scuba instructors.

Georgann and Mike have presented scores of programs to groups such as The Erie Maritime Museum, Erie, PA; New York Sea Grant, Oswego, NY; Goderich Marine Heritage Festival, Goderich, Ontario; Shipwrecks, Welland, Ontario; Ohio Council Scuba Fest; The Great Lakes Historical Society, Vermilion, Ohio; Shipwrecks and Scuba, Sandusky, Ohio; Shipwrecks Remembered, Port Huron, Michigan and Ghost Ships Festival, Milwaukee, Wisconsin.

Both are hoping to add to the more the 15 wrecks they have located in this Great Lake.

NEED ADDITIONAL COPIES?

Additional copies of *Erie Wrecks & Lights, Erie Wrecks East 2nd Edition* and *Erie Wrecks West* may be ordered directly from the publisher:

Corporate Impact
33326 Bonnieview Drive, Suite 200
Avon Lake, Ohio 44012-1230

Phone/ Fax: 440-930-2525
Email: Shipwrecks@ErieWrecks.com
Web: www.eriewrecks.com